History Workshop

History Workshop

Reconstructing the Past with Elementary Students

BY
KAREN L. JORGENSEN

WITH
James W. Venable

HEINEMANN
Portsmouth, NH

Heinemann
A division of Reed Elsevier Inc.
361 Hanover Street
Portsmouth, NH 03801-3912
Offices and agents throughout the world

We would like to thank the children and parents who have given their permission to include material in this book. Every effort has been made to contact the copyright holders for permission to reprint borrowed material where necessary. We regret any oversights that may have occurred and would be happy to rectify them in future printings of this work.

Library of Congress Cataloging-in-Publication Data

Jorgensen, Karen L.
    History workshop : reconstructing the past with elementary
students / Karen L. Jorgensen with James W. Venable.
        p.   cm.
    Includes bibliographical references.
    ISBN 0-435-08900-5
    1. History—Study and teaching (Elementary)—United States.
2. Language experience approach in education—United States.
I. Venable, James W. II. Title.
    LB1582.U6J67   1993
    372.89′044—dc20   92-42158
                                              CIP

Designed by Joni Doherty
Photographs by Karen L. Jorgensen
Printed in the United States of America on acid-free paper
94 95 96 97 9 8 7 6 5 4 3 2

Contents

Foreword
YETTA M. GOODMAN

It was a colorful autumn day in Detroit. Debi, my oldest daughter, who was then in fifth grade, came running into the house. She threw her books onto the floor in the entry hall, called out in a mournful voice, "I hate social studies," and ran up the stairs to her bedroom.

I was somewhat taken aback. Social studies was my favorite field of study. I had been a history major, and as an elementary and middle school teacher, I used concepts from the social studies as the major subject-area focus in my curriculum. My students and I debated current events and planned units of work related to important issues. We participated in firsthand experiences such as going to a courtroom to see how justice works and voting on the people responsible for running our classroom. We held mock local and presidential elections. I wanted my students to understand that they are part of history and that the major concepts of the social sciences impact their daily lives in dynamic ways.

How then could *my* daughter hate social studies? Debi participated eagerly whenever we worked on local or national elections. She was at my side during civil rights and peace marches. She participated confidently in talk at the dinner table about significant political issues. Concerned with the attitude Debi had exhibited as she came into the house, I followed her into her room. She was stretched out on her bed surrounded by her collection of Laura Ingalls Wilder books, lost *On the Banks of Plum Creek*. When Debi was reading, it was never easy to call her back from her immersion with the characters, the setting, and the action of her books.

But I did call her back from the "wheels of fire" that Laura, her mother, and a neighbor were trying to put out. "Debi, how can you hate social studies?"

Debi sighed and said: "We're studying the westward movement and the social studies book is so boring. We have to copy the dates and the places and list some main events and answer some dumb questions. Who cares?"

I reminded Debi that the stories she loved about Laura, her family, and their westward travels were part of the same historical period that she was studying in social studies. But Debi was quickly lost once again in her narrative and my "wise" words were lost on her at that moment.

I recall that scene, which took place over twenty-five years ago, whenever I hear students talk about their boring social science classes or whenever I hear teachers talking about how difficult it is to interest their students in social studies.

And I recalled that scene again as I read with great interest *History Workshop: Reconstructing the Past with Elementary Students.* My interest turned into excitement when I realized that here was a curricular concept that would actively immerse teachers and their students in the history process, bringing content and language together into a powerful transaction. Not only does the book discuss history teaching and language learning from the perspective of students taking the stance of professional historians but it provides a well-documented story about how teachers explore the role of historians with their students and how such teaching impacts the language and conceptual development of individual students.

This story about the organizational problems of, the pitfalls in, and the responses to adapting the concept of a history workshop to elementary classrooms provides a flexible framework for teachers. This book avoids establishing a regimen for the teaching of history that must be followed in a specific way. Rather, it provides prototypes and ideas that teachers can adapt and interpret to establish a history workshop in their own classrooms taking into account the strengths, knowledge, personalities, and backgrounds of their students and their families and the context of their communities. In the last paragraph of the preface, the author indicates the tentative nature of moving into a history workshop with students when she describes her work as "a progress report." In her afterword, she raises questions she's still wondering about and in so doing invites other teacher-researchers to experiment and respond.

All writing for teachers needs to assume such a tentative stance because whenever professional teachers consider new ideas, those ideas must be reflected on, interpreted anew, and put into practice in unique ways. *History Workshop* not only advocates teaching history by placing students at the center of the inquiry process but also opens new roads for teachers to explore and offers new innovations for teachers to put into practice and to study. The story of this collaboration by Karen Jorgensen, James Venable, and others provides a blueprint by which other teacher-researchers can study the theory and practice of a workshop approach to history. As more teachers participate in and write about their experiences with this dynamic new concept, the teaching and learning of history will take on new meaning not simply as part of the history curriculum but as part of curriculum development in general.

In an environment in which learners are immersed in observing and responding to artifacts, in reading and writing as it relates to their inquiries, and in presenting their ideas to others in oral and written forms, teachers will observe learners interpreting what they see and constructing new concepts about history. Understanding students' interpretations and concepts and then observing how those concepts about particular moments in history change over time will give teacher-researchers significant insights into how students use language to come to know history. Students build stereotypes or miscues about historical understanding. Placing students in settings where they have control over their own learning, where they ask their own questions based on informed observations, and where they learn to appreciate their personal connections with those who lived in other times and places not only allows students to reconsider their developing understanding but provides teacher-researchers with knowledge about how misunderstanding is reconsidered in the process of learning.

Ken Goodman and I have been saying for some time that whole language teaching is not simply a reading program concerned with the teaching of reading and writing and literature. It is a philosophy concerned with understanding the integration of a humanistic and scientific view of teaching, learning, curriculum, and language within the social nature of the educational enterprise. Whole language teachers use their expertise in a wide range of subject areas to help students perceive new learning opportunities and to engage them in self-learning and self-reflection. Since whole language is a philosophy, it's adaptable to all areas of curriculum and therefore this application of a whole language philosophy to the teaching of history will be welcomed by all teachers interested in the power of learners making connections with the past in order to understand themselves and the present.

History Workshop embodies a number of significant whole language principles. It carefully documents the role of teachers in seeding the learning environment: in offering invitations for students to participate in their own inquiry, and in negotiating curriculum. It also documents the role of students as they ask significant questions, begin to think deeply and seriously about the questions that they ask, and sense the power of their own learning.

It makes an important contribution to understanding constructivist learning principles. It provides evidence that learning in all areas of the curriculum is an active and inventive process. It allows both students and teachers to see themselves as actively involved in constructing and reconstructing historical conceptualizations. The case studies of Sandra, Elizabeth, Tanisha, and Veun not only reveal the strengths of students as they come to control their own learning but reveal the respect the teacher-researchers have for the language and conceptual development of their students.

This book shows how to provide rich and multiple opportunities for students to use oral and written language to expand and extend their learning of history. Students use new vocabulary and new grammatical structures and express new meanings as they explore history in these new ways. Through transcriptions and descriptions of classroom scenarios, this book documents how students are constantly engaged in using new language functions and forms. In the enthusiasm to involve students in using reading and writing, teachers sometimes organize their classrooms so that their students are immersed in the reading of fiction and the writing of narratives. But in addition to reading and writing for personal pleasure, students need to be immersed in a wide range of functional and authentic uses of oral and written language. In so doing students become aware of multiple ways to use language to solve their own problems and to make sense of their world.

Karen Jorgensen brings her sociopsycholinguistic understanding of the reading and writing processes and her experiences with the teaching of reading and writing to her teaching of history. Her workshop procedures include students' search for personal and social historical meaning that embodies the construction of meaning. Constructing hypotheses and new concepts through active manipulation of historical artifacts and then refining and adapting them are related to the concepts of predicting and confirming. The unique ideas students construct during such processes are shared orally during conferences or in other presentational forms; then, in their negotiations with others, students adapt and rethink ideas. They sometimes move toward socially acceptable and conventional meanings. Other times students maintain their unique responses and show through supporting evidence and growing knowledge the appropriateness of their inventive ideas. The workshop concept involves a good deal of social interaction so that students continually examine and reexamine their personal interpretations or inventions about the nature of historical ideas in light of the beliefs and interpretations of others: students, teachers, community experts, etc. Learning history, then, becomes a dynamic process always amenable to new interpretation and change depending on growing evidence and knowledge. It is active and constructive.

Another principle embedded in these history workshops is the concept of immersion—the doing of history, not some kind of abstract "readiness" to learn about history. Students and teachers organize classrooms that invite students to add to the richness of the pictorial representations, artifacts, and memoirs necessary for the workshop to take place. In such settings classrooms become studios or laboratories where serious study occurs and students find multiple ways to represent their own ideas about history.

Karen Jorgensen provides new openings for teacher and student inquiry. As teachers help their students see history as Sandra, Elizabeth, Tanisha, and Veun come to know it, then their students will see the relationship between history, literature, learning, and their own daily lives. Then students like Debi, also, will find the exploration of the artifacts and concepts of history as personally consuming as the great literature written about those historical moments. For all these students, I say *thanks* to those who have worked to conceptualize and develop *History Workshop*.

Preface

$\mathbf{F}$our years ago I wrote a letter to Cynthia Brown asking whether she wanted to collaborate on a book about teaching history. I wrote to her because I liked working with her and thought her background as a historian and as a high school and college teacher would complement my experience at the elementary level. I also respected her as a writer, having read her book on Paulo Freire and her biography of Septema Clark, which won an American Book Award in 1987. I told her I wanted to write a book that would cover the whole range of schooling, kindergarten through high school. Cynthia answered my letter with a phone call: she wanted to work on the project. We met the following Sunday morning, and again and again during the next year. Some of the ideas in the first part of this book evolved out of those Sunday morning talks. I owe a debt to Cynthia, and I hope she knows it.

In the end, a K–12 book about teaching history was too broad for a single volume, so we split the project. *History Workshop* is the end result of three years at Washington School in Alameda, California, exploring the connection between language and history teaching in the third, fourth, and fifth grades. Cynthia is working on the high school version of the workshop, which is forthcoming from Heinemann.

On those Sunday mornings we were swept by a sense of timeliness. We knew it was time to look at history teaching in a new way, to examine the "old paradigm" and to question the traditional ways of teaching history just as others had questioned the traditional ways of teaching reading and writing. And once we started looking we couldn't stop. Sometime during the year we discovered the obvious: although history was created through language, in the classroom it was separated from reading and writing and talking. But it doesn't make sense to think about history as a separate part of the curriculum. This book explores a different way of looking at teaching history—as a natural extension of language development.

Teaching is an interactive profession for me, and I can no more teach without colleagues than I can teach without students. I need to talk about my ideas and share insights with others. Janet Buckley and James Venable, two colleagues at Washington School, are an important part of this book. Janet helped plan the fifth-grade workshop, and we taught together several mornings a week for three months. She read the manuscript and gave me useful feedback during the year we worked together in her classroom. For three years, James and I struggled to implement the workshop with third and fourth graders. Sometimes we taught a lesson together; sometimes one of us taught and the other observed. On occasion, I took small groups of students to my room for quiet discussions and conferences. When I couldn't be there, James conducted the workshop by himself. During this period he offered important insights that helped me refine my teaching and clarify the theoretical underpinning of a workshop approach to learning history. He also read successive drafts of the book and contributed his expertise as a writing teacher when we encountered problems in the classroom as we struggled to redefine our role as history teachers.

Many other people also contributed to this book. Mary Robillard, Carole Chin, Matt Downey, and Yetta Goodman read and commented on the various drafts of the manuscript, and Carole Robie, my principal at Washington school in Alameda, supported my work by trusting my judgment as a teacher and as a researcher. The Alameda Historical Museum and the National Center for the Study of Writing at the University of California, Berkeley, generously lent artifacts for the history centers.

I am also indebted to Toby Gordon at Heinemann for her encouragement and her comments on successive drafts of the manuscript. I take sole responsibility for any errors or misjudgments that appear in these pages.

Finally, my thanks to Alan Huisman for efficiently guiding the book through production.

I wrote this book as a personal narrative of my teaching experiences during the past three years. I wanted to capture the struggles, the puzzling moments, and the discoveries I made working with Janet and James and three classrooms of third, fourth, and fifth graders. If the words on these pages sound tentative, it's because I'm still learning. This book is a progress report.

Introduction

During the last two decades I've watched and listened to children talk, draw, read, and write about history. In the process I've refined my own ideas about the past and learned to teach history as a process. It's difficult to reconstruct this journey, to recapture the moments when I unraveled a paradox or clarified something that confused me and saw more distinctly the connection between history and language. But somewhere along the way the idea of seeing history learning as an extension of language development became so obvious to me that I had to explore it in the classroom.

My journey began in the late 1960s when I first discovered the power of history. I was a graduate student at the University of California studying the sociology of crime and wrote a paper about the "child savers," the turn-of-the-century reformers who created the juvenile justice system. As I leafed through articles describing the work of the early settlement houses, I found myself wanting to talk to these writers. I wanted to ask them why they wished to save children they didn't know. As I looked at Jacob Riis's photographs of Russian and Italian immigrant children living in dirty little tenement rooms and working as "newsies" on the streets or in sweatshops in the garment district, I saw in their eyes a kind of weariness, a weariness that Jacob Riis must have seen too. Riis's images helped me understand the reformers, but what struck me most of all was how easily I saw into the past, how deeply I was moved by reading dusty journal pages and looking at reprinted photographs. I was hooked, and I eventually wrote a historical dissertation for my doctorate in education at the university.

But it was parenting three young children in the late seventies that led me to wonder how youngsters felt when they looked at historical photographs or read letters from women traveling overland to California in the 1850s. My children were curious about everything, and I wanted to know what they saw in those remnants of the past, what interested them, what confused them. I wanted to know how their interests and imaginations changed as they grew older. But most of all I wanted to pass on my enthusiasm for and my enchantment with the past.

After I graduated from the university, I decided to try to teach history to children by working as a volunteer in a second-grade classroom. The teacher and I planned a historical architecture walk in the neighborhood, and I brought in slides of nineteenth-century school children and early Berkeley street scenes. During the next five or six years, I spent a large part of my time working with second through sixth graders.

My work with children led to a position with the Berkeley Teachers' Center developing curriculum materials and conducting after-school work-shops for local teachers. I started the Berkeley History Project during this period and created a series of history trunks that circulated from classroom to classroom in the Berkeley schools. I left the Teachers' Center a few years later and worked as an independent consultant, writing and occasionally helping local school districts develop their history–social studies programs. When I walked into my own classroom as a teacher some eight years later, I brought all these experiences with me.

And by this time, I wanted to teach history not simply because of my own excitement about it but because I realized that as children learn about the past, they also learn about themselves. They define their own identity and place in the world. I saw this in the classroom, and I also saw it in my own life. In 1983, the year before my father died, I flew to Los Angeles with my tape recorder to interview him. I asked him questions I had always wanted to ask him: What did you think it would be like in this country before you left Denmark in 1921? Why did you marry Mom? What did you think about me when you first saw me as a baby? What was the Great Depression like? What was the most important thing you ever did? How do you want to be remem-bered? I transcribed, edited, and bound the interview, and when I gave it to him the following Christmas he started to cry. I cried too, because I knew I had done something very important for both of us. I had tried to capture the meaning of his life. He was touched by how much I cared, and through my father's story I learned about myself.

By the end of my first year in the classroom, I was convinced that history was not only an engaging activity, it was also an essential part of school experience. Recording my father's oral history taught me about my history. Without an understanding of this past, I knew I wouldn't be able to see how my ideas and attitudes have changed, how my life is linked to those of my parents and grandparents, and how I fit into the broad sweep of human history. I knew that children needed to develop this kind of understanding, and it was my job to help them.

During this period, I also learned about writing from James Venable, another third-grade teacher down the hall at Emerson, who'd taught writing in a workshop setting for years. James coached me during the day at school, and I read Donald Graves and Lucy Calkins in the evenings at home. In time, I became a better observer of children and a better writing teacher. During my second year, I ran a fairly decent writing workshop; there were many days when I sat back, listened to the hum of writing talk in my room, and watched my third graders solve their own writing problems.

Yet I still didn't see the connection between what I was learning about writing and what I knew about history. And I was always in a rush: there was math and reading and writing and music and P.E.—and maybe three forty-five-minute periods in the late afternoons for "social studies." That was the district requirement, two hours and fifteen minutes a week for something about which I felt it was so important for children to learn. I was very frustrated, and my history teaching was very directive. I created lessons on how to look at, or "read," old photographs, brought in old-timers to interview, and asked my students to write about the experiences I orchestrated. I tried to connect our studies to their lives because I knew this was important, but I didn't ask them what they wanted to study or write about.

I was so enamored of the writing workshop that I thought even then about developing a history workshop. But I didn't change the way I was teaching history, because despite the minimal time allotment, it seemed to work. (I now think my students enjoyed it because I loved it and used primary or firsthand sources instead of a textbook.) And besides, I really liked telling children about my view of history. I saw myself as a historical docent, carefully guiding my students on my tour of the past, providing them with opportunities to share what I saw in Riis's photographs, allowing them to see history as I thought they should see it. Somehow it was their job to figure out how they fit into my story.

I left the classroom after two years to become a reading teacher at Washington School in Alameda, California. I was anxious about working at Washington because it was a multiethnic school that served children from over a dozen different language groups. My new job was challenging, to say the least. The first year, I taught approximately ninety first through fifth graders. I knew I needed to know more about reading, so I spent the first few months of the school year reading Holdaway, Harste and Burke, Ken and Yetta Goodman. I used miscue analysis and developed a program that combined in-class collaboration with classroom teachers, small-group pull-out, and an extended day for some of my students. By the end of the year I had a much clearer vision of how readers make sense out of what they read and what I needed to do to help them.

But I never stopped thinking about history. It was sometime during this year that I started to apply what I was learning about reading and writing to what I knew about history. I realized that learning about history, like learning to read and write, was a process in which children create or construct personal and social meaning. I also began to see that historical learning didn't just happen at school, it didn't end after a six-week history unit, and it didn't end in June. History learning was a complex, long-term quest for identity— a search for personal and social meaning—that never ended. It all sounds so simple to me now, like something I should have known all along. But I didn't know it, because I didn't understand how children acquire language and how language is connected to communication and thinking. Yet it was this revolutionary idea that made me rethink my whole approach to teaching history.

It also seemed timely. I sensed that other teachers were ready too. After all, the California state curriculum framework called for "writing across the curriculum" and more integration of history–social studies and the language arts. Many of my colleagues implemented writing process and holistic approaches to reading. And some of them—including me—were bored with the never-ending pet, Disneyland, and Nintendo stories that came out of writing workshop. Why not apply what we knew about reading and writing process to teaching history? Why not think about learning history as a process?

PART ONE

Learning History as a Process

Learning history is an ongoing process in which children construct historical meaning as they talk, read, write, draw, and reflect. Through language, they propose and test historical ideas by predicting, confirming, and negotiating with others. They weigh new ideas against what they already know about the world, their own purposes, their understanding of relevant historical source materials, and the responses of other learners.

The historical meaning they create—theories about how long ago events occurred, how events are sequenced in time, how events influence each other, and what makes an event historically significant—helps them to define their personal identity and construct social meaning in everyday life. They also construct ideas about different historical milieus. All of these insights are interrelated and refined from day to day.

The history workshop is a studio setting in which learners discuss the meaning of artifacts, oral history transcriptions, historical photographs, and other firsthand sources from the past. Teachers participate by facilitating interactions between children and by playing the role of elders, guiding younger learners as they explore a variety of historical writings.

In the pages that follow, I examine parallels between the history process and the reading/writing/thinking process and outline what I believe are essential elements of an effective history workshop.

. . . .

Children's Historical Understanding

Children create for themselves an understanding of the past. I suspect that these insights are in a constant state of flux, that children are almost always in the process of testing their hypotheses and refining their ideas. Many fifth graders openly discuss chronology and attempt to refine their sense of the sequence and duration of events. I tape-recorded some wonderful examples of students' talk in Janet Buckley's fifth-grade classroom at Washington School. We were studying life in the United States at the turn of the century and had set up several "history centers" containing historical artifacts. I also put out fifty to sixty historical photographs for the students to browse through.

At one of the centers Terry and Allen were talking about chronology. When I listened to them discuss an 1887 photograph of a woman from Illinois, I was struck by their references to time. They constantly referred to "then" and "now."

TERRY: Looks like my grandma . . .

ALLEN: Looks like Joey's grandma!

TERRY: She's pretty, for an old lady.

ALLEN: They looked hecka funny then.

TERRY: She's hecka funny in those days . . . she's hecka funny now."

ALLEN: Yeah!

TERRY: She's probably walking on a cane now.

ALLEN: (*Picks up an 1887 photograph of an older woman*) She's ugly now, look at this, now she's all ugly!

TERRY: (*Points to original photograph*) That's her then. (*Points to Allen's photograph*) That's her now.

ALLEN: They're all dead, I guess.

How long ago did these women live, and how are their lives linked in time? As the boys talked, Allen decided that neither of the women was still alive. They continued their conversation for a few more minutes, revising from one moment to the next their beliefs about the age and longevity of the women in the photographs.

Children also try to understand how historical events influence one another. I recorded an interesting example in James Venable's room at Washington School when five of his third graders discussed Native American customs and attempted to sort out the relationship between going to the sweathouse and going hunting, two important Ohlone activities. In the course of their conversation, Billy, Veun, Carl, Christina, and Pete never reached a consensus, but they did struggle to create a plausible relationship between sweathouse rituals and hunting behavior.

VEUN: The sweathouse was where men could make arrows and bows in the sweathouse and to sweat.

CHRISTINA: If they didn't want to eat that ocean stuff, they would have to go to the sweathouse and stuff and go get some deers.

VEUN: Why did they sweat in the sweathouse?

PETE: To relax.

CARL: No.

BILLY: To get their toxics out.

MR. VENABLE: Why do you think they wanted to do that?

BILLY: I don't know. It might have polluted their bodies?

Eight- and nine-year-olds establish criteria for deciding whether or not an event is historically significant. Joan, a third grader in James's class, wrote two personal narratives, one in September and one in October. The September piece (Figure 1–1) was about a family trip to her Aunt Robin's house in Santa Cruz; the October piece (Figure 1–2) was about the 7.1 earthquake that occurred in the Bay Area on October 17, 1989.

MS. JORGENSEN: Can we talk about your earthquake story for a moment? Do you think that your story will interest other kids in the class?

JOAN: Maybe.

MS. JORGENSEN: Why?

JOAN: Maybe some of them were, like, not living here at the time or having a vacation. They might want to know what is was like here, if they just felt a little wherever they were.

MS. JORGENSEN: Have you written other stories?

JOAN: Yes, one about my trip to Santa Cruz.

MS. JORGENSEN: Which one of your two stories do you think is the more important?

JOAN: My earthquake story because it was telling something that happened and it was really serious.

MS. JORGENSEN: And your Santa Cruz story?

JOAN: No, because all it was was just me going somewhere.

MS. JORGENSEN: Does the Santa Cruz story tell us about history?

JOAN: No because twice during the summer I go to Santa Cruz, and I usually do the same things.

MS. JORGENSEN: What about the earthquake story?

JOAN: Yes, because there will probably never be another one like it.

MS. JORGENSEN: So to be history, something has to be . . . ?

JOAN: Like, something that happens, that sort of like happens to a big part of the world.

MS. JORGENSEN: Have you ever thought that things that happen to you are a part of history?

JOAN: No, well it might be a part of history to my family or to me, but the world—it's not, because it didn't happen to everybody.

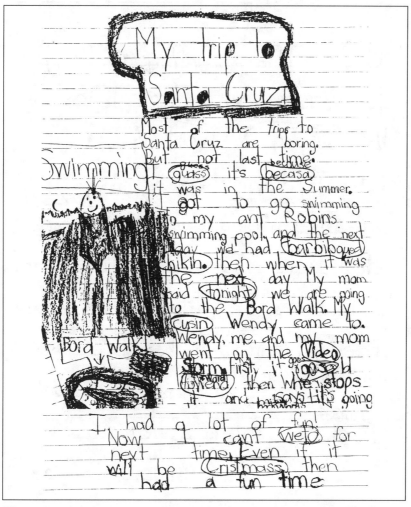

Figure 1–1

Children try to understand how people lived during different historical milieus—the settings or environments for historical personages and events. I like to use the term *milieu* because it's less precise than the term *historical period,* which is often defined by historians according to adult criteria, such as cultural, technological, or commercial changes, that have little meaning for young people. When children construct historical milieus, they use their own criteria. They frequently define modern times by the presence of inventions like cars and electricity and then demarcate older milieus according to dwelling and clothing styles. The ten-year-olds I've interviewed use these criteria to describe a number of old-fashioned settings, including cave dwellers/dinosaurs, medieval castles, the primitive tropics, pioneers, cowboys and Indians, Pilgrims and Indians, pirates, and a vague turn-of-the-century

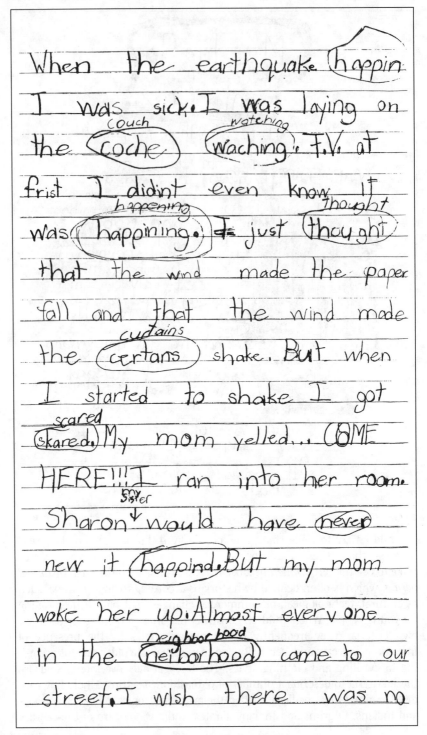

When the earthquake happin
I was sick. I was laying on
the coche [couch] waching [watching] T.V. at
frist I didint even know It
was happining. [happening] I just thought
that the wind made the paper
fall and that the wind made
the certans [curtains] shake. But when
I started to shake I got
skared. [scared] My mom yelled... COME
HERE!!! I ran into her room.
Sharon↓ [my sister] would have never
new it happind. But my mom
woke her up. Almost every one
In the neiborhood [neighborhood] came to our
street. I wish there was no

Figure 1–2

era delineated by old-fashioned cars and early electronic technology. These historical settings seem to rely heavily on the images children have seen in movies and television.

I became acutely aware of the kinds of historical milieus children construct when I watched James's third graders draw an Ohlone village for our American Indian workshop. Before they started, we told them that the Ohlones were Native Americans but gave them no other information. In their drawings, they sketched and colored images of Plains Indians wearing headbands and feathers, living in teepees, and killing buffalo (Figure 1–3). They drew what they currently knew about this time and place, lumping the Ohlone with undifferentiated "Indians" in a milieu largely based on media stereotypes.

Children's historical understanding changes over time, although it's unclear whether this change occurs in distinct linear stages or if it is a highly individualized, unpredictable process unique to each learner. Although there is little sound research on this issue, for some children long-term development probably goes something like this: "Billy," a bright and curious four-year-old, lives in a timeless, ahistorical world in which images of the past—both real and imagined—are indiscriminately interwoven with the present. By the age of seven or eight, his concept of "past" and "present" is fairly distinct. He listens to stories about the Ohlone Indians, plays with their gambling sticks and arrowheads, and examines a drawing of a village shaman. He realizes that these people lived "a long time ago," but he's confused about how long "a long time ago" is and he doesn't seem very interested in the question. Historical chronology means little to him.

His understanding of the Ohlone milieu is a hodgepodge of Plains and Eastern Seaboard Indian cultures derived from mass media stereotypes. Like the third graders, he draws teepees, bows and arrows, and hunters in fringed deerskin clothing and moccasins. For him the Ohlone milieu is similar to these other milieus. And in the corner of one of his pictures, he draws something fascinatingly unexpected: a hunter shooting arrows at a bull's eye. For Billy, the anachronism makes sense—after all, wouldn't he practice with a bull's eye if he were a Native American hunter?

Billy understands that historical events are related to each other, but he doesn't see the connection between his life and the life of the Ohlones. For him this exotic culture is somehow detached from the present. It's difficult for him to understand how a shaman who lived two thousand years ago is in any way related to the Alameda he can touch, hear, smell, and see. He doesn't sense the broad sweep of human events that connects his life to this ancient Ohlone village.

At ten, Billy shows increased interest in historical chronology and sees some connections between his life and the life of people in other times and places. At seventeen, he understands that the Ohlones flourished two thousand, not fifty, years ago and sees more complex connections

Figure 1–3

between events and ideas. He understands the practical reasons for the sweathouse—that it was important for the men to get rid of their own scent before tracking animals. He also comprehends the relationship between hunting and the spirit world, understanding that the sweathouse served as a chamber where the hunter cleansed his soul as well as his body.

He may even take his thinking one step further to reject the TV stereotype of Native Americans and describe a number of Indian milieus, putting himself into a drawing of Ohlone life and feeling what it was like to gather and hunt in the San Francisco Bay Area when wildlife was abundant. He may empathize with the shaman, understanding his powers without comparing his healing practices with those of modern medicine.

And perhaps by now, he also sees connections between his life and the life of the early Alamedians and perceives the sweep of history in which

Figure 1–3 (continued)

the Ohlone past is interwoven with his present. As he looks at the almost birdless sky, he reflects on his image of the Ohlone horizon, darkened with huge flocks of cormorants and wild geese. He may even see connections between the Ohlone milieu, nineteenth-century Germany, and Alameda in 1993.

Constructing Historical Meaning

Learning history is an ongoing process in which children construct historical meaning in the same way they construct meaning when they read and write. They make sense of whole text by devising and confirming predictions and they construct historical understanding by placing events and ideas into a meaningful context and predicting and confirming new ideas in dialogue with others.

CONTEXT

In learning history, as in reading and writing. children require meaningful contexts. It took me a long time to see the similarities between decontextualized skill-drill reading/writing instruction and decontextualized skill-drill history teaching. Date and event "knowing" is like word and sound "knowing." Both approaches decontextualize knowledge and neither one necessarily leads to understanding.

I discovered the link between skill-drill history instruction and skill-drill reading instruction by watching youngsters struggle to construct meaning from isolated sounds and words. Wendy, a second grader in my program a few years ago, was a good example of a child who knew her "letters and sounds" but couldn't read. At the beginning of second grade I interviewed her about her reading. She told me that she didn't like books very much, even though her grandmother read to her daily. Listening to Wendy read was painful: sound for sound, word for word, she plodded through a selection and, at the end, retold almost nothing. She was a classic example of Margaret Phenny's "underpredictive reader" who learned to "read" by participating in a set sequence of isolated phonics lessons.

It was hard to know exactly what transformed Wendy into a self-confident reader by winter vacation. A large part of the credit goes to her classroom teacher, who allowed her to read self-selected books for long periods every day. Her grandmother also helped by modeling reading for her, and Wendy herself never quite gave up—she was a spunky little girl who quietly persevered despite her small size and timidity.

Wendy and other beginning readers need a context in order to create meaning out of the abstract symbols of language. When Wendy explored books she wanted to read, she discovered that there was meaning in Arnold Lobel's *Frog and Toad Together* and in Pat Hutchins's *Rosie's Walk*. She discovered that these stories had a meaning greater than the sum of their words.

Wendy and young historians like her also need a context in order to create meaning or make sense out of isolated historical events and dates. I confess that I used to teach history the way Wendy's first-grade teacher taught reading. Perhaps one of the worst things I did was to ask my students to make timelines. Asking them to list events along a line representing "time" was asking them to take events out of historical context and strip them of meaning. The American Revolution started in 1776. The cotton gin was invented some years later. So what? When used alone, timelines are the epitome of skill-drill history. Children can't comprehend historical meaning by sequencing isolated and decontextualized dates any more than Wendy can make sense of text by knowing a sound or a word.

PREDICTION AND CONFIRMATION

Children construct historical meaning by making and confirming predictions as they talk with others. Predictions are the hypotheses that children test by weighing new ideas against current ideas, what they know about the world, their own purposes, their understanding of relevant historical source materials, and the responses of adults and peers.

I struggled with these ideas. I knew children used language in constructing their understanding, but I wasn't sure how they went about it. Did they construct historical meaning from diaries, nineteenth-century flatirons, and historical photographs in the same way they constructed meaning when they read George Seldon's *Cricket in Times Square* or Esphyr Slobodkina's *Caps for Sale?* What were the parallels between making sense of stories and making sense of historical sources and historical writing?

I had my first breakthrough when I listened to children talking during the first week of Ohlone artifact exploration in James's class. As I walked from group to group, I heard students trying to identify the Native American items placed in the history centers around the room. They wrangled and argued about the grinding stones, arrowheads, and clapper sticks. At one point, Christina came to me and announced that the clapper stick was a fishing pole. Her guess was a prediction.

It was also an "unexpected response," not what I thought she might say. In a way, these unexpected responses are the miscues of historical thinking. Just as Wendy's reading miscues were not "errors," Christina's unexpected historical response wasn't a "misconception" about the past but a window into her thinking, a quick glimpse at her historical understanding of Native Americans. Unexpected historical responses parallel reading miscues in another way. Children make and confirm predictions in a social setting, and in the process of talking with others they evaluate the appropriateness of their unexpected responses according to a group consensus about what makes sense. When Wendy read "hats" instead of "caps" it made sense to me and to most of her peers. No one said anything or tried to "correct" her because the group came to an unspoken consensus that Wendy's miscue made sense. We shared a tacit understanding about the range of words that readers might meaningfully substitute for "caps" within the context of the story. If Wendy had substituted "clapped" for "cap," however, she would have received a different response. I think the group would have agreed that "clapped" didn't make sense. And if we negotiated with her and she still insisted that "cap" was "clapped," we'd move on, trusting that she would probably share our discomfort with her substitution as she continued to read and reflect.

Likewise, when Christina predicted that the clapper stick was a fishing pole, it didn't make sense to me. I know about fishing poles: some are made out of bamboo like the clapper stick, but they're longer. And I expect to see some evidence of a fishing line, at least a notch where one could be tied. If I gathered together a group of students who also knew how to fish, they would quickly come to the same conclusion. We share an understanding of "fishing poleness" and the range of objects that can reasonably be placed in that category. We would come to the consensus that you couldn't catch a fish with the clapper stick. And if the group knew enough about Native Americans in California, they would also object to Christina's prediction because of their shared belief that the Ohlones fished with nets.

Children make different types of predictions when they first encounter unknown artifacts or other firsthand sources. Younger children tend to make descriptive predictions, wishing to classify unfamiliar artifacts or to describe how they are made and what they look like. This is what Christina did: she predicted that the clapper stick belonged to the object category "fishing pole." By fifth grade, some children make interpretive predictions spontaneously and speculate about the meaning of a historical diary entry or attempt to date an artifact or an old lithograph. This is what Terry and Allen did when they discussed the age of the woman in the 1887 photograph.

Christina might be able to make an interpretive prediction with a little help. In our discussion, I would ask her to think about what the clapper stick meant to the Ohlones. Her prediction would constitute an interpretation of the artifact's function, just as Wendy's understanding of the meaning of *Caps for Sale* is an interpretation of the author's purposes. What is the author saying to us? What does the clapper stick tell us about Ohlone life? What do the story and the artifact teach us about ourselves? If Christina's response didn't make sense to me, I'd be honest and offer mine, but I wouldn't insist that I was right. There are no "right predictions," no "misconceptions," only sensible interpretations of the past.

Creating a Workshop Setting

A workshop setting functions like an artist's studio. Students explore historical source materials, read a variety of historical writings, draw, make up stories, and recreate historical experiences by comparing their understanding with that of others. The firsthand or primary sources provide the raw material for predictions, while reading and writing stories and drawing offer a context for weaving isolated predictions into a meaningful whole. Teachers are the master artists or the elders of the workshop, offering their views about the past and encouraging interactions and negotiations between learners. I want to say more about firsthand sources, stories, drawings, and the negotiation process because these elements are so important to the success of a history workshop.

FIRSTHAND SOURCES

Historical photographs, artifacts, and memoirs are the paint and canvas of the history workshop, the raw materials of historical understanding. Without them, our sense of the past would be based only on speculation and our understanding of the present. An 1862 photograph of a nearly deserted Union army camp helps us recreate a scene from the Civil War, a scene we can't experience directly. The photograph helps us "see" firsthand the thick canvas tents, the weary look in a straggler's eye, the mud, the ruts in the road left by the wheels of long-gone artillery and supply wagons, the dead chilliness of the early morning hour. The photograph allows us to "be there," to reconstruct this experience from the past so that we can find meaning in it.

In a studio or workshop setting, primary sources, especially photographs, oral histories, artifacts, diaries, and letters, become the "manipulatives" of history teaching. Like Unifix™ cubes, they provide a tangible means of imagining the abstract. Pretending to scrub laundry on a turn-of-the-century washboard helps students understand women's household chores in 1905 in the same way that geodesic blocks teach them about edges and faces.

I've experimented with a number of firsthand sources over the years and have found that artifacts or historical objects, visual images like photographs, oral history interviews, and some written materials stimulate the thinking of young students. Each type of material provides a different kind of information about the past and a different way of testing hypotheses.

Artifacts are the most "concrete" of all firsthand sources. They provide students with the kinesthetic experience of touching, using, and smelling an object from a historical milieu. They represent contemporary resources and technology and are good sources of information about technological change and everyday life. I try to use artifacts in the workshop, especially during the first few days, allowing ample time for students to examine and role-play with old cameras, period clothing, and strange objects from other times and places. They spontaneously classify unknown artifacts into familiar object categories, predicting that hooks for buttoning nineteenth-century shoes are crochet needles and that Mexican mantillas are head scarves. Most third graders have difficulty going beyond these descriptions, while some older students automatically date and compare artifacts from different historical milieus.

Historical photographs, lithographs, paintings, and film footage offer visual images of the past that are particularly useful for confirming predictions. Historical photographs show real people wearing period clothing and using objects contemporary with that period. They give these objects a social context and provide information to help students refine their ideas. And these resources are fairly easy to find: photographs are available for many post-1850 milieus, and paintings and lithographs remain sources of visual information for earlier historical settings. Commercial films documenting major events or offering glimpses of big city street life after the turn of the century are also available.

Oral history provides an additional opportunity for students to confirm and revise their understanding of the past. Oral history interviews are interactive sources of information that offer students a chance to talk directly with persons who lived in other historical milieus. Did they have McDonald's back then? Did you have to sit in a corner of the schoolroom when you were bad? Did you ever wear pants when you were a little girl? Were you very poor during the Great Depression? Children often need to hear someone "from the past" respond to their questions in order to evaluate their predictions.

Written sources are the most difficult firsthand materials to use with young children. Diary entries, letters, memoirs, and transcriptions of oral history interviews are rich in information, but they are often hard to read. Women's diaries of the journey west in the 1850s, for instance, provide accounts of hardships on the trail but their archaic vocabulary and sentence structure are difficult for modern readers. Students find it hard to make predictions from these materials unless the information is presented as drama: readers theater, role plays, or tape-recorded interpretive readings.

READING AND WRITING STORIES

It's not enough for students to evaluate their predictions about the Civil War while they listen to letters written by Union and Confederate foot soldiers or explore other firsthand sources in the workshop. They also need to synthesize these predictions into a meaningful whole. Reading and writing stories forces young thinkers to place isolated and seemingly disparate ideas into context and encourages them to refine their understanding and sensibly recreate a milieu.

Reading History Stories

Not long ago, I sat with two eight-year-olds, Oscar and Carlos, talking to them about Elizabeth Shub's *The White Stallion,* a story about a young girl who wandered away from an Oregon-bound wagon train in the 1850s. Carlos's and Oscar's understanding of a "pioneer" milieu emerged as we conversed.

MS. JORGENSEN: When do you think this story took place?
OSCAR: Back on a farm.
MS. JORGENSEN: When?
OSCAR: I don't know.
MS. JORGENSEN: Make a guess: today, a long time ago . . . ?
OSCAR: A real long time ago.
MS. JORGENSEN: How about you, Carlos. What do you think?
CARLOS: A long time ago.
MS. JORGENSEN: What makes you think it took place a long time ago?
OSCAR: They have wagons that horses pull.
MS. JORGENSEN: What else?
CARLOS: They have horses working instead of cars.
MS. JORGENSEN: What about the characters? What about them?
CARLOS: They wore different clothes.
MS. JORGENSEN: Can you describe the clothes?
CARLOS: They wore cowboy clothes and hats.
MS. JORGENSEN: What else did you notice in the story that tells us about this time?
CARLOS: They used hay for the horses.
OSCAR: They made houses out of pieces of log and slides out of wood, lots of things out of wood. And metal and plastic.
MS. JORGENSEN: What plastic things do you remember from the story?
OSCAR: (*Long pause*) None, I guess.
CARLOS: Nothing. It was a long time ago.

Reading stories also helps children take isolated predictions about the past and begin to see how historical events are related. In another conversation, James explored this process while discussing Elizabeth Coerr's *Sadako and a Thousand Paper Cranes* with three third-grade boys. The story is about Sadako, a child who dies of leukemia in 1954 because of the atomic bombing of Hiroshima.

CARL: What were the Japanese doing to the Americans?
BILLY: They were going to attack Pearl Harbor.
MR. VENABLE: They had already attacked Pearl Harbor.
CARL: Then we dropped a bomb. Did we drop an atomic bomb?
MR. VENABLE: Yes.
PETE: Because Japan wouldn't surrender.
MR. VENABLE: Some people think that that was the reason.
BILLY: My dad said that Japan was trying to rule the world.
MR. VENABLE: Some people think that, too.

PETE: How many people died like Sadako?

MR. VENABLE: I don't know exactly, but thousands of people died.

CARL: There was a show on TV, a show on the Japanese war, when they dropped the bomb. It showed when they dropped the bomb and what happened. They showed in the show a lady who was in Japan when they dropped the bomb. She was still alive and she was old. And she told about what happened, and they tried to make it look like just what the book said.

MR. VENABLE: Was the show like the book?

CARL: A lot of the stuff was. A lot of it.

Through their discussion, the boys began to weave their ideas into a meaningful theory. The story provided the framework, stimulating them to link the dropping of the bomb to the causes of the Second World War.

Writing History Stories

Writing stories also forces youngsters to put their predictions into a context. Editing my father's oral history helped me to understand this idea in a very personal way. The meaning of his story began to emerge as we talked, but it was even clearer later as I shaped a string of isolated anecdotes into a narrative. How did the experiences of a ten-year-old boy crossing the Atlantic on the *U.S.S. United States* in 1921 fit with the life of a newly married high school football coach in Mt. Shasta, California, in the mid-1930s? As I edited the interview, I created a story out of his words and, in the process, refined and clarified my understanding of his life.

I've observed children write about history in a number of genres. During our Native American workshop, we asked students in James's third grade to write history stories. Almost two thirds of them wrote realistic historical fiction set in Ohlone times; the other third wrote historical fantasy, informational pieces, and personal narrative. I was struck by this because James had introduced the writing by suggesting that they think about Ohlone life and write a realistic story, drawing from their reading and their experiences at the artifact centers.

Carl's piece is a good example of realistic historical fiction. He mapped his story first, analyzing his characters, his setting, and his plot. His map (Figure 1–4) reminded me of the analytical approach he took to the artifacts during his explorations at the history centers and showed me that he had a sense of the genre, although later in his writing he had difficulty in working out a story problem. Carl's interest in the arrowheads at one of the centers surfaces in his lead sentence:

The Rain God has Arrived

One morning Brite Sun awoke and heard some kind of noise coming from outside. He went quietly outside and saw his father Cloud Rain carving arrowheads out of obsidian rocks.

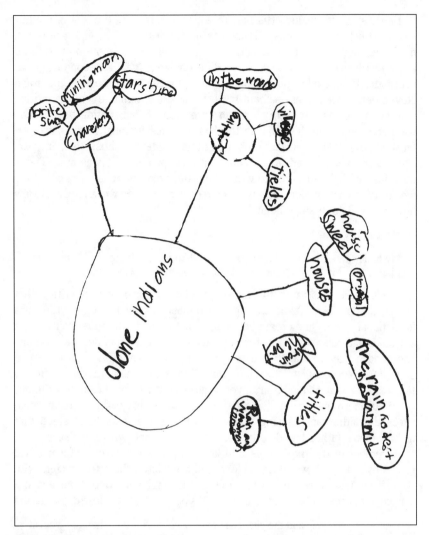

Figure 1–4

Lisa's piece is very different. She and six other students wrote stories we called historical fantasy, which contained the basic elements of fairy tales. Lisa's story, for instance, is set in "once upon a time." Sweet Rose, the innocent heroine, has lost her way in the forest and is confronted by the reputedly evil Moonlight. Later in the story, Moonlight turns into a good witch who uses her magic powers to help Sweet Rose. In Lisa's words, Moonlight "did a spell on her so her knee would not hurt." Her *Magic Indian* piece starts like this:

> Once upon a time a little girl named Sweet Rose she was wondering around in the forest. She was going to go pick flowers and shells. A while later she was lost and she hurt her knee. She was crying and crying until a lady named Moonlight came. . . .

Ben's story is unique. His narrative about fishing in the sea is neither historical fiction nor fantasy. He wrote in the first person, like a personal narrative. Ben was struggling in this piece, trying to figure out how to write a story with characters who spoke "a different language." A second language user himself, he explored personal narrative for the first time in October and November, writing stories about trips, friends, and family events in writing workshop. His Ohlone story was an extension of this writing because he used an event from his past as the basis for his fictional story. After he finished, Ben, along with a number of other students, chose to write personal narratives instead of a second historical piece. This was fine. These students needed more time to write about their experiences. We knew they would try to write fiction again but would do it when they were ready. Here's how Ben's Ohlone story begins:

My Family and I

My family and I drove to San Francisco. When we got there my brother and I had a net. My brother said, at a different language, "There's a starfish."

Ben's piece illustrates the autobiographical nature of the writing that emerges from the workshop. Many children use personal events as the basis for fictional stories and create characters that embody the personality traits of friends and relatives. The story becomes an extension of personal experience and a way to clarify and redefine identity. Sometimes children use stories to solve conflicts. Joan's second Ohlone piece is a striking example. It is a story about Shining Star, a young girl who runs from her mother to get the medicine man for her dying father. In Joan's story, the medicine man saves the father and Shining Star is "so happy that she didn't sleep that night." Joan's father had died two months before she wrote her story.

A number of the third graders in James's classroom wrote informational pieces even though we made it clear that we wanted them to struggle with the difficult task of reconstructing the past through narrative. Louisa wrote a piece about the Ohlone customs the class had discussed a few days earlier:

Indians are very big and the girls can't make any houses and when the woman get pregnant the man can't touch the woman for two years and the men go to the sweathouse and they make arrows and they go out to hunt . . .

Children often write informational pieces when they have a choice of genres. When James and I talked about this, we concluded that realistic historical fiction was an important genre in the history workshop but very difficult for some students to write. Most authors used their own experiences as the basis for their stories and drew on personal narratives and fairy tales as structural models. Others opted not to write stories at all but to work on pieces that were more like descriptive exposition than narrative.

When children write informational pieces or stories about a particular historical milieu, they often focus on different aspects of the milieu because they draw on different personal experiences and have different interests. As they talk with one another, however, they expand their view of the setting beyond the limits of their own piece. Many writers network frequently during a workshop, talking, writing, and immersing themselves in further information about the milieu. Christina learned the details of making acorn mush when she responded to Pete's Ohlone family story and Pete learned more about Ohlone folk medicine when Carl asked him to help decide which healing plant Foxwalker should use to reduce his son's fever. From day to day, children rethink their ideas as they seek advice and respond to other writers.

Because reconstructing the past is a social process, I encourage students to look for the connections between their pieces during whole class discussions in which we map the historical information in our collective writing. I also publish a class magazine that focuses on the milieu. Each contribution to the magazine or to the discussion becomes a component of a historical collage; each piece becomes a part of a greater whole. The combined works uniquely reconstruct a small sliver of the past and represent the larger context of our shared understanding of a historical time and place.

Each writer who contributes to our shared understanding also becomes an authority, a historian in his or her own right, and a participant in the process of reconstructing the past. They each contribute what they can. Some construct long, intricate stories clearly set in the historical setting; others produce pieces filled with anachronisms, inconsistent details, and other unexpected responses. Some choose to create small private stories about children playing games or getting sick; others struggle to recreate large public events involving inventions or wars that have changed our lives. Some continually rethink their historical understanding; others are less active. Not everyone in the room "masters" every concept, but all the children write and think at their own pace, in their own way, and for their own purposes.

DRAWING

Drawing pictures of historical milieus lets students place disparate and isolated predictions into a meaningful context. History drawings help children clarify their understanding in the same way that illustrations help them identify and refine other ideas. As a writing teacher I've watched young writers discover a story by visualizing characters and story events as they draw. The narrative seems to take shape as they organize space and add details and color. This is especially true for young children, who don't separate the story in their pictorial symbols from the story in their alphabetic symbols, for whom the illustrations tell an unwritten part of the story or complement the written text. Likewise, as a history teacher I've observed children discover new historical meaning as they draw. In their illustrations, they synthesize their predictions and visually symbolize their understanding of the past.

NEGOTIATING MEANING

Children construct historical meaning within the social setting of the workshop by negotiating with others as they write narrative, represent milieus in their drawings, read, and talk about history. Each negotiation is a social transaction in which students rethink their ideas in response to the reactions of other learners. Negotiations in the history workshop occur within student/teacher transactions and within student/student transactions. In student/teacher transactions, the teacher plays the role of master artist or elder. In student/student transactions, the teacher plays the role of facilitator.

Negotiations Between Students and Teachers

As a teacher I have the power to dominate social transactions with students. In a workshop this power is a problem, because students can't construct their own historical ideas unless they are empowered to disagree with mine. At the same time, I don't want my voice to dominate the dialogue. I want to be a colearner. So I've learned to acknowledge that I'm not the only authority. I've learned to be an elder, a more knowledgeable learner who guides younger students as they discover new ideas and refine their sense of history.

But it's hard to balance power relationships with students, to see myself as an elder and not as an authority. It's difficult to relinquish ownership of history and allow my students to see the past through their own experiences. I loved those photographs by Jacob Riis. And my father's stories of the Great Depression profoundly altered my images of the 1930s. I can't be dishonest and pretend they didn't. So I've had to find ways to share my ideas without insisting that my vision of the past be my students' vision of the past.

Ownership issues are fairly easy to solve when student talk, draw, and write stories based on firsthand experiences, about things they already "own." It's their experience, and my job is to help them clarify what they know and tell their story well. I had an "ownership struggle" with a student during my second year as a third-grade teacher. Bobby came into my room virtually unable to write more than one sentence. By early November he had a few short voiceless pieces in his writing folder. But something happened to him around December. I remember watching him, head down, writing intensely for four or five days, nonstop. At the end of the week he asked for a conference and quietly handed me a long, disorganized piece on the World Series. My first response was total joy: he had made a breakthrough! I praised his fluency and proceeded to talk with him about how his piece was organized.

Now I think I probably rushed in too quickly. Bobby resented my suggestion that he think about rearranging his story. He took my comments as mandates and decided that I didn't really mean what I said when I told the class that they made the final decisions about their writing. He put his piece away and stopped writing for two weeks. At first I was frustrated. What a stubborn kid! Why couldn't he see that his piece was disorganized? Then I realized we were having an ownership struggle and the only way both of us could win was for me to let him do what he wanted, hoping that sometime later he would think about my advice.

A week later he brought his work back to me. He had revised it. It was a stronger piece, better organized, more focused, although it was far from perfect. In fact, I really wanted him to rethink it again, but I backed off. I knew I would have other opportunities to help him strengthen his writing, and I wanted to convey the message that I respected him as a writer and that he was ultimately in control of his work.

Ownership issues are more difficult to solve when children write history. The problem arises because we experience the past indirectly and own only our contemporary understanding about events in other times and places. Billy and I can't experience the daily ritual of an Ohlone family, but we can imagine it and reconstruct it by touching gambling sticks, by reading a missionary's diary, by talking about an anthropologist's drawings of an Ohlone village, by reading how other historians viewed Ohlone life, by drawing a boat made out of tule reeds, and by writing an Ohlone story. Unlike Bobby's experience watching the World Series, neither of us owns the Ohlone past. But we do own our understanding about the Ohlones, and we negotiate these ideas with each other and with peers. By talking with each other, we discover and refine our ideas about the Ohlones, using the available resources, our prior ideas, and our current understanding of the world. We negotiate the meaning embedded in artifacts, visual images, and other surviving remnants of the Ohlones and, in the process, we each create our own unique view of this historical milieu.

I avoid dominating this transaction with Billy by remembering that I'm not the only historian in the classroom, that I might be wiser but I'm still learning. As a more knowledgeable colearner, I research ideas and write stories with my students, using my example as a model of thinking and risk taking. When I struggle with my lead, complain about the limits of our history library, or wonder where I'm going next with my piece, I demonstrate that uncertainty and discomfort are an important part of learning and that we are grappling with the same problems.

I also keep from dominating my negotiations with Billy by carefully monitoring what I say. It's too easy for him to believe exactly what I believe because I'm the adult, "the teacher." After all, I've read more than he has about the Ohlones and the California missions and the Civil War; and over the years I've developed a broad understanding of historical chronology, significance, and the relationship between historical events. But I try to use this experience to guide him to discover his own meaning, not to force him to adopt mine.

When I speak to Billy as a guide, I try not to cut off his thinking and imagining. I encourage him to conjecture and construct meaning freely and then as time goes on help him to reexamine his interpretations. I try not to "tell" him what to think but to model thinking: to demonstrate how I believe something works, to validate his predictions, to point out seeming contradictions, and to help him confirm or disconfirm his theories. As an elder, I've learned to say: "What makes historical sense to me is . . ." instead of "This is the way it was"; "Some historians think . . ." instead of "We know that . . ."; "How do you know that?" or "Does that make historical sense?" instead of "You're wrong."

I also try to stress that we will have more questions than answers and that our answers are always tentative. What did the author of an 1859 letter written on the Oregon Trail mean when she said, "This is no pleasure trip upon which we have idle time hanging upon our hands"? What makes you think that? Why does the clapper stick have a hole at one end? Does that make sense? What do you see in this photograph? Do you see something different from what I see? Why do you think we see it differently? In each conversation, I learn a little more about Billy and reveal something about myself. Over the course of the year, I encourage Billy and the other students to trust their own responses, to see that there is no one way to interpret a historical letter, no single truth to discover in the pages of a historical diary or in the images of a turn-of-the-century photograph, no formula for writing about the past.

I also maintain my role as guide and elder by constantly evaluating my interactions with students. Am I allowing them to explore sources freely and make predictions without overly directing these experiences? Do I encourage them to talk with one another even more than they talk with me? Do I accept unexpected responses as I accept meaningful miscues and encourage students to create ideas about historical settings that are different from mine? Do I trust that in the long term, as we continue to negotiate, most of their unexpected responses will evolve into something that makes more sense to me, although they may not necessarily mirror my own understanding?

Negotiations Between Students

The understandings students negotiate through interaction with one another are as important, if not more important, than those they negotiate with me. Students test their predictions and refine meaning in the workshop when they talk with one another, when they collaborate to describe and classify artifacts, when they talk about historical photographs, work in small groups, browse in the history resource library, read historical fiction, or draw or write a story.

When students negotiate with one another, they often engage in spontaneous role playing and analytical talk. One of the most striking examples occurred in Janet's fifth-grade classroom during the first week of the workshop, when students were exploring artifacts, including the items at a center filled with kitchen gadgets from 1900. The conversation began like this:

MARIA: (*Points to waffle iron*) That's a waffle maker.
ALI: (*Picks up meat grinder*) Hey, what's this?
IAN: Coffee maker again.
MOSTAFA: Don't stick your hands in there.
MARIA: (*Opens a tea tin*) Tea bags.
SOPHIA: (*Holds coffee grinder*) Look at my coffee. It's black. That's a neat grinder.
IAN: (*Points to stove-top toaster*) This is a toaster.

ALI: No it isn't. It's a grater.

MARIA: It's a cheese grater.

IAN: It is?

MARIA: Yeah.

IAN: . . . 'cause I've had toast from it, at lunch. See, they would set the toast here.

MOSTAFA: (*Picks up french-fry cutter*) What the heck is this?

ALI: Don't cut your hand.

MOSTAFA: I know. You put a potato in here, and it's french fries.

MARIA: You put [the waffle iron] over a fire like this.

MOSTAFA: There're your french fries.

ALI: That's weird, the waffle maker.

MARIA: (*Still holding waffle iron*) Anybody need to put butter on here? Anybody?

SOPHIA: Let's see the tea bags. Okay. Look at those tea bags.

MARIA: (*Pretending to hold a milk pitcher*) This is milk. Anybody want milk?

MOSTAFA: (*Picking up the meat grinder*) Another coffee grinder, Ian?

IAN: No, it's a meat smasher.

MOSTAFA: What do you do? You just put meat in these?

ALI: (*Looking at the meat grinder*) I bet it's a pasta thing.

IAN: (*Continuing to talk about the meat grinder*) I know what. It's a flour grinder.

At this point in the discussion, Maria, Mostafa, and Sophia begin to role-play, while Ali and Ian continue to analyze the artifacts:

Role Play

MARIA: Let's play house. Let's play house, old-fashioned days. Oh, what's in here? Some tea? Anybody want to come to my house? Okay, it's good to see you.

SOPHIA: Want some tea? Would you like some tea, dear, some tea?

MOSTAFA: Yeah, we'll, I'll have it tomorrow.

SOPHIA: Tomorrow, dear. We'll have tea tomorrow. Should buy some tea then. See, it says (*Reads off tea tin*) you should buy a package tomorrow.

MARIA: So we must call to the grocer because we don't have any tea.

MOSTAFA: Yes, and I will go to the store, madam.

MARIA: Tea, anyone?

Analytical Dialogue

ALI: (*Holding nut cracker*) It's a cracker. It's a nut cracker.

IAN: Feel how heavy these bottles are.

ALI: Smell [the bottle]. Smell it. It smells just like iron.

IAN: What color is this [bottle]?

ALI: It's a little dark brown. This one's, ah, I don't know, green, could be green.

I've listened to hours of student-to-student history talk, and it strikes me that some children prefer one type over the other, although most use both kinds when they negotiate with one another. I am not sure whether this can be explained by gender, learning styles, or situational influences. My guess is that all three factors come into play when students are allowed to explore on their own and at their own pace. Many of the girls I observed preferred role playing, although—as Maria illustrates—some girls used analytical talk as well. Ian and Ali never pretended during their conversation at the kitchen gadget table but were actively role-playing at the turn-of-the-century-clothing center the next day. James and I talked about these apparent language differences and wondered whether students who tended to role-play would have an easier time developing a historical narrative later in the workshop. This turned out to be true in some cases but not in others.

I've also observed children assume roles when they negotiate with one another. Some children initiate predictions, offering a hypothesis for the group to negotiate. Others take on confirmation roles by echoing, elaborating, or refuting a prediction. Still others play the observer, watching the interaction but not overtly participating in the dialogue. Terry and Allen's interchange (page 3) at the historical-photograph center illustrates how this role playing works. When the two boys discussed the woman in the 1887 photograph, Terry initiated the predictions and Allen confirmed them by elaborating on Terry's ideas. As I listened, I heard two related discussions in their one-minute dialogue: at first they discussed what the woman looked like in 1887; then they began to wonder what she looked like today and whether she was still alive. Terry initiated the first negotiation with a prediction that the woman looked like "my grandma." Allen elaborated by responding that the woman also looked like "Joey's grandma." After a few seconds, Terry initiated the second discussion by suggesting that the woman was "hecka funny in those days. She's hecka funny now." Allen again responded with an elaboration of Terry's idea by picking up another photograph and offering, "She's ugly now, look at this, now she's all ugly."

Student negotiations provide an open-ended, unpredictable, and non-threatening testing ground for predictions. I don't think that Terry and Allen would have told me that the woman in the historical photograph looked "hecka funny," but they felt free to say so when I wasn't around. Their discussion took on a kidlike quality as they laced their talk with images of old ladies walking with canes. Allen and Terry truly owned this conversation, and there was no way for me to know in advance that they would conclude their negotiations with a comparison of "now and then."

As I've learned, I don't need to control all of the student history talk that goes on during the workshop. My role in student/student transactions is to facilitate negotiations between students by providing them with opportunities to talk to one another. When I set up history centers during the first week of the workshop, for instance, I establish rules for sharing the artifacts and orchestrate rotation from center to center, but I don't intrude into student conversations. If they ask me to identify an artifact, I turn the question back to the group and continue to listen. And I don't worry about the unexpected responses students generate when they talk to each other, because I know that we can negotiate some of these ideas as we discuss the artifacts later in the workshop.

THE TEACHER AND THE CURRICULUM

In suggesting that children construct their own meaning from a historical event, I know I'm bucking the tide of mainstream history teaching. What about developing citizens for a democracy—isn't that important? What about teaching our multiethnic heritage—isn't that essential? The California State History–Social Science Framework clearly articulates an approach to history that I feel obligated to incorporate into my teaching. Suggestions for the curriculum include page after page of understandings about the past, classified into strands and with major concepts printed in bold type. The course descriptions tell me in detail which times and places I need to emphasize.

I have to confess that I worry about "covering the curriculum," and I know that principals, colleagues, and parents worry about it, too. I feel pressured to ensure that third graders leave third grade with an understanding of community history and that fifth graders leave fifth grade with an understanding of United States history. And I'm not suggesting that we throw out the framework any more than I'm suggesting that I refrain from sharing my own view of history with my students. But my views, the state framework, and the district's curriculum should serve as a checklist, not a prescription.

The history workshop is a compromise between the competing interests of a child-centered classroom and the mandates of state and district frameworks. In James's classroom, we compromised by choosing workshop topics that fit the state guidelines and bringing in most of the books, artifacts, and other resources to support these studies, but we also fostered student ownership by encouraging youngsters to contribute additional resources, to choose their own writing topics, and to freely explore our history centers. And many students did share artifacts and photographs: Kathy added a Native American headdress to one of the centers; others brought in old family photo albums or odd items from the back of the garage. When I look at the Ohlone magazine produced by James's students and the 1900 milieu reconstructed by the writers in Janet's fifth grade, I also see a variety of student-selected topics and genres.

In both classrooms our thinking was refined from day to day. If we were to continue this process through high school, our historical understanding would evolve from workshop to workshop and from year to year in a never-ending cycle of exploration and rethinking. Over the long term, each child would develop a unique set of ideas, and, as a group, we would "cover the curriculum" in spite of ourselves.

PART TWO

The History Workshop

I begin the history workshop by encouraging students to write personal narratives. I've learned to see these experience-based stories as a form of history writing, and, for young children, I consider them a natural bridge to other historical genres. To initiate the study of a particular milieu I set up artifact centers around the room. I encourage students to discuss and negotiate the meaning of the artifacts and then ask them to put their understanding into context by making a drawing of the milieu.

After an initial period of exploration, I add new resources to the history centers and share my own views about the past, trying to help learners examine their hypotheses as they renegotiate the meaning of firsthand sources. The exploration of these sources continues as students write stories about the milieu. Throughout the workshop, I encourage the students to read historical stories as well.

In the pages that follow, I show how I talk with students to stimulate them to think historically about personal narratives, interact with book discussion groups to help clarify important issues related to historical writing, handle student/student and student/teacher negotiations at the history centers, and conduct drawing conferences. I also describe the shared understanding that emerges from the workshop and explain how I encourage storywriting through minilessons and conferences.

• •

The First Year's Experiment

I first experimented with the workshop a few years ago in James's third and fourth grade combination class. We aligned our studies with the district framework by focusing on nineteenth-century California. Since we knew from the outset that the workshop would involve some kind of exploration of firsthand sources, I brought in my California photographs and artifacts and we arranged them in several centers around the room. All the photographs went into one center, and I put twenty or so slides in a projector and taped a paper screen to the wall so students could view the slides on their own.

In another artifact center I put a reproduction of a porcelain doll, a piece of Irish lace, an old tobacco tin containing marbles, and children's books from the 1880s. A third center contained diary excerpts and other written sources, including a letter from a woman traveling to California in 1859. In another corner of the room, I placed a handmade Chinese doll, a small herb scale, and a photograph of a Chinese woman who came to California at the end of the nineteenth century.

As small groups of students rotated from center to center, we watched what they did. They seemed interested in the photographs and the artifacts but for the most part ignored the written sources. Even when I taught minilessons highlighting items at this center, I never got more than a luke-warm response to the old letters and diaries.

Then James walked the class through a group writing of a story set during the California gold rush. The children wanted to write a mystery, and they chose the story problem, created the characters, and wrote the piece together during a series of class meetings. We expected that this experience would help them use the resources at the centers to write their own stories, but their individual pieces were disappointing. Most of the students wrote short, flat narratives with little plot or character development and, for the most part, they didn't connect what they experienced in the centers to their writing.

But the vision was there. I knew we could apply the writing workshop model to teaching history. It was going to take time, and we needed to experiment and explore the questions that came up during that first year. How much modeling of storywriting do students need? Should I begin the year with historical genres and continue to have children read them through-out the workshop? Should I model how to write by writing with them? Maybe I needed to slow the process down, and allow more exploration time at the centers. We sensed that the children needed more time for ideas to percolate and for negotiations with peers. But how much time was enough?

And what was my role in the workshop? I wondered about my confer-ences. That first year I'd tried to step back and offer ideas. Should I be more explicit about what made historical sense to me? How could I negotiate with the students so that they felt they still owned their writing? How could I help them negotiate with one another? And how could I use their writing and their talk to assess their understanding? How could I tell when their understanding changed?

Then there was the problem of the centers. How could I get them to use the resources, to see the connection between the artifacts, the diaries, the photographs, and their stories? I spent the next year struggling with these questions, trying to solve the problems of story modeling, pacing, negotiating, and assessing understanding and to discover how to get students to use historical resources to help them write and think.

Personal Narrative as History

I begin a history workshop with a "Donald Gravesian" writing workshop that emphasizes personal narratives. It's relatively easy for students to write about their own experiences, and I want them to feel comfortable about taking risks in their writing. Within four or five weeks, most students realize that I trust them to make decisions about their work.

I also like to begin with personal narratives because they are a form of history writing and provide young children with a natural bridge to other historical genres. As a writing teacher I'd often thought of pet and trip stories as autobiographical vignettes—short but memorable stories from a child's past. As I developed the history workshop, I saw the connection between personal narratives and history. Shouldn't writing about historical events in their own lives help them write about events they hadn't experienced directly? Couldn't children use these experiences as the basis for their fictional writing? And if I asked them historical questions, wouldn't they see their stories in a new light? At the very least, I knew that listening to children talk about their writing gave me information about their historical understanding.

I encourage students to think historically about personal narratives by asking them historical questions when we talk about these experienced-based stories. Jimmy's conference illustrates how this kind of dialogue helps children begin to understand chronology, how events are related, and what makes them significant. I talked to him during the same week I talked to Joan about her trip to Santa Cruz and her earthquake story, so I was particularly interested in what he had to say: Jimmy had also written an earthquake story and a story about his trip to see his relatives in the Philippines.

In many ways, Jimmy's Philippines piece is a typical "bed to bed" trip story. He narrates event after event and ends his story when he flies home to the Bay Area. His concern with chronology, however, is striking: both his title and his lead tell us that he went to the Philippines during the summer. He also specifies the month and the year of his trip. In the body of his piece he refers to "time" on five occasions. He seems particularly interested in telling us, almost hour by hour, what happened after the train derailment. The events in this section of his piece are clearly delineated by time.

When We Went to the Philippines This Summer

A Trip to the Bicol Region
In the summer of June 1990, we went to the Philippines. It was hot there. When we drank water, it was always boiled because the water tasted different there and if you didn't boil the water you would feel funny! And if you did boil the water, you would feel normal.

One night when we went somewhere far from our home, we rode a train to a place called Bicol Region, but instead we ended up in a place called South Super Highway because the train jumped off the track.

When everyone was sleeping in the train, suddenly the train made a big jolt, and then everybody woke up. We saw that the tracks were broken. The conductor said that the lights were going to go out. Two cars were detached. The train went backwards. Then our car went off the track. We got our luggage and went to the other car in the back. Then the train went backwards to a train station.

It was 2:03 AM when we got there. The train went backwards to another place. Then we rode the taxi to where we stopped before. Then we got home at 3:00 AM. We slept for five hours. We woke up at 8:00 AM to catch a plane!

A Trip to Another Place

When we got to Naga, we stayed there for five weeks to swim in a pool called Monte Cuss. We swam in the pool everyday.

Then we went to a place called Legaspi. That's where I got most of my pants and clothes. Then we went back to our home in Manila.

Back Home

Then we rode a plane back here. Then we waited in the airport until my dad arrived. Then we went home to eat lunch.

His earthquake story is particularly poignant because his aunt was killed when the 880 freeway overpass collapsed in Oakland. He was in the middle of the earthquake story when I interviewed him. In our conference, Jimmy and I talked about time concepts.

MS. JORGENSEN: Are you going to revise your earthquake piece?

JIMMY: Maybe. One thing I have to add is the time. When it occurred.

MS. JORGENSEN: How can you find that out?

JIMMY: Well, I know it's about 5:12. My mom was preparing the food then. I said, "The water is shaking!" I thought it was ghosts, but ghosts don't exist. . . .

MS. JORGENSEN: How long ago was your trip to the Philippines?

JIMMY: Oh, about a year ago. No, about two or three months ago.

MS. JORGENSEN: How old were you then?

JIMMY: I was seven.

MS. JORGENSEN: How old were the others in your story?

JIMMY: I don't know much about their ages. I do know one thing, that, you know, today is the 23rd, right? Well, if I were in the Philippines right now it would be the 24th because it's a different place and a different time—it's like morning right here so it'll be night over there. It rotates, the world rotates, so the time is different.

To get Jimmy to think about how events are related to each other, I asked him how his trip and the earthquake changed his life:

MS. JORGENSEN: How did your trip change you?

JIMMY: Well, it felt strange. Like there were *Archie* comic books there and then my cousin said that there were some in America. Then when I got back, a bookstore opened and, oh boy, I saw the *Archie* books.

MS. JORGENSEN: So how would you be different if you hadn't taken this trip?

JIMMY: Well, I would be the same person as in second grade. Like when the train in the Philippines jumped off the track it called my attention to being scared. That was one of my most important events, so I wrote it down in my story.

MS. JORGENSEN: How did the earthquake change you?

JIMMY: I never felt different, but maybe I did feel different, and I just didn't know.

MS. JORGENSEN: How did your aunt's death affect you?

JIMMY: It affected me because when we had the funeral, everyone was crying, and my other aunt next door, she cried. I cried really hard because I really liked her. I loved her.

Toward the end of our conference, Jimmy and I talked about the importance of these events. Like Joan he separated events into personal history and public history, believing that for events to be historical they have to be "unique." While Joan believed that an event had to happen to everyone, Jimmy took a *Guiness Book of World Records* approach.

MS. JORGENSEN: Was the earthquake an important event?

JIMMY: It was, because lots of things happened. My auntie died and some people also have died that I don't know and their feelings have changed somehow. It affected me and my dad and my mom. It was my dad's sister who died.

MS. JORGENSEN: Is the earthquake event a part of history?

JIMMY: Maybe. It's in second place of all the hardest earthquakes in history. Because it was kind of hard and maybe the 1906 earthquake was a bit harder and this one was a bit lower.

MS. JORGENSEN: Any other reason?

JIMMY: It happened in more than one place. The 1906 earthquake was just in San Francisco, might have spread to Oakland. But in 1989 it was here and it spread to Santa Cruz and Oakland and San Francisco.

MS. JORGENSEN: What about your trip to the Philippines? Is that history?

JIMMY: No.

MS. JORGENSEN: Why not?

JIMMY: Because it doesn't have any important events like most of history does. Like if you did something that nobody can do—like—this didn't really happen—like you throw a heavy bowling ball up and it falls on your head and you don't die and that's history. It's amazing, that's why.

MS. JORGENSEN: So the earthquake was history because . . . ?

JIMMY: . . . it was amazing.

MS. JORGENSEN: Was your other story history?

JIMMY: No, but it was important to me.

Throughout the year, I encourage children to read historical narratives because books serve as models for writing and sources of information about the past. I provide time for students to read independently or to work in self-selected small groups. Sometimes I read aloud to the whole class; at other times I help individual students use the history library to research specific questions. Depending on their needs, students browse through a variety of writings or focus on a particular book or subject. I like to start this "history reading" early in the school year.

In James's room that fall, we began by asking students to read a historical novel as a small discussion group. They could chose from seven books: *Sadako and a Thousand Paper Cranes*, by Eleanor Coerr; *Sarah, Plain and Tall*, by Patricia MacLachlan; *The White Stallion*, by Elizabeth Shub; *Anna and the Big Storm*, by Carla Stevens; *A Lion to Guard Us*, by Clyde Bulla; *Stay Away from Simon*, by Carol Carrick; and *White Bird*, by Clyde Bulla. Children found some books, like *Sadako*, challenging to read; others, like *The White Stallion* and *White Bird*, were much easier. The books covered a wide geographic and chronological span: *Sadako*, for example, was set in Japan in 1954 and *A Lion to Guard Us* in seventeenth-century England and Jamestown, Virginia.

We wanted to give James's students as much ownership of their reading as possible. He suggested that we rotate the book sets from table to table and allow each group time to browse. James gave a minilesson on browsing and after a few days asked the class to write their first, second, and third choices on a slip of paper, hoping to form small groups of readers interested in the same book. This worked fairly well, and James set up the groups and distributed the books. For the next week or so, students spent about an hour a day reading and discussing the stories. Usually they read their selection independently for thirty minutes and spent the rest of the time talking about their ideas in small groups or with the whole class.

With small discussion groups, I try to raise issues that will help children explore history and examine the different ways authors write about it. In one group, James talked about how the author of *Sadako and a Thousand Paper Cranes* based the book on a true story but invented some of the details in order create a logical plot:

MR. VENABLE: Is *Sadako* historical fiction?
PETE: Well, it could be historical because they had atom bombs back
    then, and it might not be because I think they still have them.
MR. VENABLE: How about the rest of you? What do you think?
BILLY: I don't know.

TIM: I don't know. Well, kind of because it was based on a true story but the writer put some things that weren't true in it.

MR. VENABLE: Like what?

TIM: Like the person probably put things in that didn't really happen. Like, I don't know if they said the exact words. Like, "Leukemia, that's impossible!" "Get up sleepy head, it's Peace Day" and stuff like that.

MR. VENABLE: You're saying that the story really happened, but the author had to make some things up that she couldn't find out about?

TIM: Yeah, that's what I meant.

MR. VENABLE: Do you think that writers of historical fiction have to make up some things that they can't find out about?

PETE: Well, I guess they would kind of have to because they don't know it.

TIM: Yeah, they don't know about everything.

MR. VENABLE: What do you think, Billy?

BILLY: That person that writes *Sadako* didn't know what to say so I guess they had to pretend about it, about what Sadako said, and her mother.

As Tim and the other students in his group discovered, writers of historical fiction frequently invent what they don't know. James talked with another group about this idea, but the children couldn't imagine writing about an event they hadn't experienced.

VEUN: If this book is about 1796, how can it get to us? He'd [the author] be dead.

MR. VENABLE: Clyde Bulla, the author of *White Bird,* is still alive today.

LEE: Wow, he's probably old!

MR. VENABLE: Why do you say he's old?

LEE: (*Sits silently*)

BRADLEY: Well, he could have written it a couple of years ago.

MR. VENABLE: Do you think the author was alive when this story was written?

LEE: No, I think he passed it on.

JEFF: I think that he might have got married, and he passed it on to his son, and his son died . . .

BRADLEY: . . . and he passed it on . . .

LEE: Oh, yeah.

MR. VENABLE: So you think that they passed the story on from one generation to the next, and someone wrote it down and made a book out of it?

LEE, JEFF, BRADLEY: Yeah.

MR. VENABLE: Could it have been written in any other way?

JEFF: I don't think so. How could he know about it?

BRADLEY: They just passed it on.

With these small discussion groups, we often explore how authors show us that a story is set in a particular historical milieu. James talked about this issue with the group reading *White Bird:*

MR. VENABLE: Did this story take place a long time ago or in modern times?

JEFF: A long time ago.

VEUN: 1976.

JEFF: '96?

LEE: 1796.

MR. VENABLE: Do you think I was alive then?

JEFF AND OTHERS: No.

MR. VENABLE: What does the writer do to tell us that this story took place in 1796?

VEUN: It said so.

MR. VENABLE: If it hadn't said it, what else in the story lets you know it took place a long time ago?

BRADLEY: The pictures are, like, hecka old. The houses are different and stuff.

MR. VENABLE: What else besides the pictures lets us know?

VEUN: . . . because Luke finds a baby in the river.

MR. VENABLE: How does that let us know that the story took place a long time ago?

VEUN: I don't know.

MR. VENABLE: Was life different back then?

JEFF: I think so.

MR. VENABLE: How can you tell from the story?

JEFF: No cars . . .

BRADLEY: They rode on the horses.

LEE: They rode like on a cart and horses pulled it.

MR. VENABLE: Anything else?

JEFF: No stop signs.

BRADLEY: They didn't have any school.

MR. VENABLE: What causes you to say that?

BRADLEY: Luke just read the Bible, that's all. They didn't have any schools. He just stayed home.

BEN: . . . and they didn't have any machines. They had horses and stuff.

We also explore this issue by discussing story problems. Margaret, Christina, and Tanya talked with me about the setting and the story problem in *Stay Away from Simon*.

MS. JORGENSEN: Tell me what this story is about.

MARGARET: It's about Simon. Everybody thinks he's bad, but he's really nice like a regular person. And one day Simon follows the girls and copies what they say, and then there's a snowstorm, and he teases them and they get lost, and he tries to take them home but the father comes on a horse. So they bring him home for dinner, and then when [one of the girls] comes down to give him some cider, she finds out he learned to count because he never learned it in school and then she thinks he's not so bad.

MS. JORGENSEN: So what's the story problem in *Simon?*

CHRISTINA: That Simon was like a devil, but they found out that he wasn't.

MS. JORGENSEN: What do you think, Tanya?

TANYA: I don't know. Yeah, I think so.

MS. JORGENSEN: How about you, Margaret?

MARGARET: I think it's about how people get to like him. But he was sort of nice at the beginning and he wasn't always good because he would do stuff. He threw snow in their hair. At the end, he gets all good. At the first part, he was sort of good.

MS. JORGENSEN: How did the author solve the problem? Did Simon change or did the other people start to see him differently?

CHRISTINA: Lucy and Josh were the first ones to know that he wasn't that mean. I guess they found out, and they didn't think that at first. They thought he was a devil.

MS. JORGENSEN: Do you think that this problem could have happened in modern times?

MARGARET: It could because people can change. The only thing that couldn't happen would be their clothes and stuff like that. Like the things they do, the different things like the lessons in school. But all the rest, it could have happened.

MS. JORGENSEN: Does this make sense to you, Christina?

CHRISTINA: I think so. It's a good story.

MS. JORGENSEN: I think Margaret is saying that even though the author lets us know by the lessons in school and the clothes the characters wear that this story takes place a long time ago, the story problem about kids learning that somebody isn't really mean could take place at other times. Is this what you mean, Margaret?

MARGARET: Yes, that it's old-fashioned but kids can change.

MS. JORGENSEN: Could this problem happen at our school today?

CHRISTINA: Yeah, like kicking kids.

TANYA: We have kids like that.

MS. JORGENSEN: What about you, Margaret?

MARGARET: I think that it happens like that.

Reading continues throughout the workshop. I try to select read-aloud books to sketch in information about a milieu and to serve as models for writing. During the time the class was exploring the artifact centers, James read two books about Ohlone life, each day ending the workshop with everyone in a circle on the carpet. He read stories from Terry Knope's

The Adventures of Little Bird and Malcolm Margolin's *The Ohlone Way,* an informational book written partly as narrative. The students chose sections for him to read and then discussed them afterward. As the workshop progressed, children spontaneously drew *Little Bird* scenes in their milieu drawings and incorporated story problems from *Little Bird* and *The Ohlone Way* into their writing.

Negotiating the Meaning of Artifacts

After they have spent several months reading history and writing personal narratives, I ask students to discuss what they know about a milieu and set up artifact centers around the room. I encourage children to talk about the artifacts, exchanging ideas with one another as they rotate from center to center. I listen to their dialogue but do not offer ideas about the artifacts. If students ask me about an item, I redirect the question with a simple "What do *you* think it is?" because I want students to explore their understanding with peers before they discuss their ideas with me.

I usually ask students to write what they know about a milieu in a history response log. We introduced the logs the first year thinking that they would provide a convenient place for children to write down the information they gathered from the centers and to express their reactions. We didn't respond in the logs ourselves. Sometimes students answered questions we had asked orally; at other times they wrote what they wanted to write.

I tried the logs again the next year, but with mixed results. Some children loved them, writing profusely, carrying them from center to center, and referring to their collected notes whenever they wrote a story or an informational piece. Others scribbled short, voiceless phrases and ignored the logs for days at a time. I'm not quite sure why this happens, but the logs seem to work for only half the children I teach. Perhaps I benefit the most, since the children's responses provide daily information that helps me plan conferences and minilessons.

Before James's students explored the Native American artifacts on display at the centers, we asked them to write down what they knew and what they wanted to know about the Ohlones. In a class meeting we talked about their ideas. Some students understood that the Ohlones lived off the land in a natural setting. As Pete put it, "There were lots of dirt, sticks, and rocks around, and they lived near the ocean and got their food from the trees." Kathy, Lisa, and a number of other students, however, pictured a milieu filled with responses we didn't expect, including "farms," "old wood schools," "little radios," and "cowboys." The questions they asked gave us further insight into their understanding. Pete wanted to know whether they had money and wrote in hieroglyphics. Kathy was curious about whether there were earthquakes in Ohlone times, and Lisa asked, "Did they really wear feathers in their hair?"

James and I talked about these responses. It seemed most of our students knew only TV stereotypes of Native Americans. Kathy's cowboys and farms and Lisa's question about feathers came from media images, from movies and television programs showing Indians confronting European settlers in the latter half of the nineteenth century. We knew how deeply embedded these stereotypes were, and it left us wondering how we could help students see the Ohlones as a rich and distinct culture.

After we discuss the response logs with the children, I put artifacts on tables around the room. The first year we noticed that if we put out everything at once, the amount of information in the diaries, photographs, oral history transcriptions, and other resources simply overwhelmed most of the students. We needed to slow things down, reduce the load, and allow more time for exploration. So we decided to change the centers a bit, and let students explore one type of source material before we introduced another. This might sound very controlling, but it turned out to be an important way of slowing the pace of the workshop.

To me it makes sense to put out the artifacts first. I've used such historical items with children for years and know that porcelain dolls and flatirons stimulate talk about history. But I had never observed students' spontaneous interaction with these objects. This was an important learning experience for me. It was easy to tell them about the Ohlone artifacts: they would listen politely and retell the story. But I needed to learn not to dominate the dialogue. Listening to their questions and their spontaneous remarks about the artifacts is a way for me to discover what they know and how they view the milieu. This helps when they try to solve their writing problems later in the workshop.

The second year James and I put together five Ohlone centers. One contained native plants, shells, nuts, and seeds that the Ohlones used for cooking, medicine, and hygiene. Another contained five or six animal skins. Gambling games and cooking utensils were among the items at two others. At the fifth, students could listen to a tape of James telling Ohlone myths.

The students examined and discussed the artifacts with each other for five days. We looked and listened as they tinkered with and talked about the various objects. We also captured student talk by putting a tape recorder in one of the centers. We knew that if we stood nearby, they would say what they thought we wanted to hear. I think at times they did perform for a tape they knew we would listen to after school, but I sensed that they often forgot about it and talked to each other as if we were not there.

Victoria, Christina, and Nicole gathered at the center containing a bark doll, a gambling game, a clapper stick, shell necklaces, and similar artifacts.

CHRISTINA: A doll!

NICOLE: A doll, look.

CHRISTINA: (*Picking up a gambling stick*) How did they use them?

VICTORIA: (*Picks up two other sticks and strikes them on another part of the counting game as if it were a xylophone*) Like this, something like this.

NICOLE: This is their doll.

CHRISTINA: (*Looking at Victoria "playing" the sticks*) They break.

VICTORIA: (*Continues to "play"*) This is what I'm going to try.

NICOLE: Look at this doll. It looks like Freddy Krueger.

CHRISTINA: (*Holds shell necklace*) What are these, guys? Oh, you can get these in Hawaii.

VICTORIA: It goes like this (*continues to "play" with the sticks*).

NICOLE: Let me play it, turned over (*turns the counting sticks over and "plays" with Victoria*).

CHRISTINA: (*Picks up clapper stick*) Put your finger in here. (*Puts finger in the hole and then blows in the hole*) See. I know! This is for fishing. We went fishing once. We fished in the afternoon and in the mornings. Because all the fish are gone after that. There were lots of fish there. I saw a fish this big. Look.

VICTORIA: Want to catch a fish or something?

CHRISTINA: Got one! It's a long one. Want to take it out?

VICTORIA: Let's cook it.

In this transaction Christina and Victoria initiate most of the predictions, while Nicole confirms them by echoing and elaborating on their ideas. The girls use analytical dialogue and role playing to negotiate the meaning of the artifacts. Christina, for instance, analyzes the possible functions of the gambling sticks; Nicole puts clues together and decides that the bark object is a doll. They are role playing when Christina says she's caught a long fish and Victoria suggests they "cook it."

This interchange between Nicole, Christina, and Victoria illustrates what happens when we slow the pace of the workshop down and allow students to explore on their own, pretending and analyzing without our intervention. We don't need to direct the role play. It happens spontaneously. We don't need to ask the girls what they think the artifacts are. They ask these questions themselves. They explore and develop their own hypotheses. I can negotiate with Christina about the "fishing pole" later. For now, her unexpected response gives me information about her understanding of the Ohlone culture. And allowing her to make her own predictions gives her the important message that her thinking is valuable. The history workshop tells her that she is a historian in the same way the writing workshop tells her that she is a writer.

After a period of artifact exploration I ask students to try to draw the historical milieu we are studying, hoping that they can begin to synthesize their ideas into a meaningful whole. By this time in the workshop, they've had plenty of time to talk with each other and make predictions, to analyze and role-play with the artifacts displayed in the centers. And I've had time to listen as they negotiate the meaning of these items and to assess their understanding of the milieu and of history in general. Drawing lets them put their historical ideas into a visual form and lets me evaluate how their understandings are changing.

MILIEU DRAWINGS

I ask students to draw a milieu, and then I confer with them about the details in their pictures. The first time I used this technique in James's classroom, my plan was to draw for only one session—but one session turned into three because the children were engaged and we were learning so much. On the first day I led the class through a visualization of what they might see if they could take themselves back in time and walk through an Ohlone village. I asked them to pretend that they were birds looking down at the village from a mountain. I wanted to find out what they saw, so I chose my words carefully, guiding them through the village but not saying anything about what I visualized. I asked them to picture the village, a family, a duck hunter, and a father. After a few minutes, they folded a sheet of paper into four sections and started to draw. James and I quietly circulated around the room while the students drew their pictures.

Most of the drawing conferences last five or ten minutes, depending on the child. I ask simple, open-ended questions aimed at stimulating story ideas and eliciting more information. When I conferred with Kathy about her picture (Figure 2–1), she began by describing the milieu, focusing on the variety of "tepees" in her Ohlone village.

Ms. JORGENSEN: Tell me about your drawing.
KATHY: This is a tree and thunder coming at it. And then the Indian watching everything. There's the tepees and the little doors they go in. And then I made the sky with the sun coming out of it. There's a different house made of straw for the little baby Indian. There's a hill that the Indian—the mother is standing on the hill and rocks are coming down and she's about to fall because the rocks are pushing her down and she didn't know they were there.
Ms. JORGENSEN: So what happens next?
KATHY: Well, the baby starts crying and the mother tries to get it. And then she gets it and it's okay.

Ms. JORGENSEN: And then?

KATHY: That's the end.

Ms. JORGENSEN: Tell me more about the tepees.

KATHY: There's this little tepee where the boys go in. And that's the girl one. They have boy and girl tepees so they won't fight. They have this "M" one; the dad and the mom live in there. Here's a little pot so the mom and dad can drink out of it.

Ms. JORGENSEN: What are the tepees made out of?

KATHY: This one is wood. That square one is made out of sticks and the "M" one is out of rock and mud.

Ms. JORGENSEN: Where did you get all these ideas?

KATHY: Out of my head.

When "There's a hill that the Indian" turned in midsentence into " . . . the mother is standing on the hill and rocks are coming down . . ." I recognized this transition from description to story and encouraged her to develop the narrative. When she decided the story was finished, I went back to eliciting information about her understanding of Ohlone life. I was particularly curious about her odd assortment of "tepees" and the gender-segregated occupants. When I probed further, she told me what they were made of but, like so many third and fourth graders, she couldn't articulate the source of her ideas. Some of them, like the triangularly shaped boys' tepee, clearly came from TV. Kathy, like most children in the class, watched television daily and even if she didn't realize it, what she saw became a very real part of what was in her "head."

The next day I talked to Nicole. Her milieu drawing (Figure 2–2) looked very different from Kathy's. As we conferred, I found out that her sense of Native American life also came from television, but she had incorporated a number of artifacts and a scene from *The Adventures of Little Bird,* which James had read and discussed with the class the day before.

Ms. JORGENSEN: Tell me about your drawing.

NICOLE: Well, I drew the Moon Lady picking up a magic leaf. I drew the wolf because it was nighttime. The wolf was bleeding and these others are laying around the fire. This is my house. They're tepees.

Ms. JORGENSEN: Are you in this drawing?

NICOLE: Yes, this is me by the fire.

Ms. JORGENSEN: Why did you put yourself in this drawing?

NICOLE: I don't know. I just wanted to be in it.

Ms. JORGENSEN: Tell me more about the designs on your tepees.

NICOLE: This has two lines of stripes. Some have raindrops. Some have birds. These are thunder. Rainbows and circles.

Ms. JORGENSEN: Where did you get these ideas?

NICOLE: I don't know . . . from my head.

Ms. JORGENSEN: Tell me more about the people in your drawing.

Figure 2–1

NICOLE: Well, the daughter is making up vegetables. The son is drilling
 holes, and the father is testing out a bow and arrow. This is the mom.
 She's making a doll.
MS. JORGENSEN: What else?
NICOLE: That's all.
MS. JORGENSEN: Where did you get these ideas?
NICOLE: That was stuff on the table. Like the drill.

Figure 2–1 (continued)

Ms. JORGENSEN: What are the people wearing?

NICOLE: The mother has kind of slippers. They have shirts like these (*Points to her shirt*) but they aren't. Everybody has feathers in their hair like hats.

Ms. JORGENSEN: What do you mean that they have shirts like these but they aren't?

NICOLE: I think they're made out of animals, like fur.

Figure 2–2

While the fur clothes, feather hats, and tepees came from the movies, Moon Lady, the wolf, and the magic leaf were borrowed from *Little Bird*. Nicole's drawing also included the Ohlone drill, the redwood doll, and arrowheads from two centers in the room. And some of the designs on the tepees looked very much like designs on the gambling sticks at the games center. Nicole wasn't sure where all her ideas came from, but her drawing showed that her experience in handling the artifacts and listening to the story had changed her ideas about Indians.

Father

hunters cotching duck

A Duck

Figure 2–2 (continued)

My talk with Nicole made me wonder whether other students in the class had drawn themselves in their Ohlone pictures. I found that seven other children had included themselves. Nicole drew herself as a participant, but the others made themselves observers, sometimes standing on a mountain overlooking the village. When I talked to Angela about this, she said she was "just watching" (Figure 2–3). Kathy said that she didn't draw herself in her picture because she "wasn't born then." Perhaps some children, like Nicole, have an easier time putting themselves in the picture because they don't see

Figure 2–3

a clear distinction between past and present. I wondered how Nicole's apparent ability to imagine herself as an Ohlone would affect her writing.

Fifth graders rarely put themselves into their pictures. Not one of Janet's students drew him- or herself on the streets or in the school houses of their turn-of-the-century towns. When I asked them about it, they told me what Kathy told me—they didn't put themselves into the picture because they were not alive then. The fifth graders clearly separated past from present,

Figure 2–3 (continued)

reality from fantasy. They had a much keener sense of chronology than many of James's third graders and more clearly understood that ninety years separated 1900 from the present. It made little sense to them to draw themselves in another time period. And when I conferred with them about their pictures in general, I heard fewer unexpected responses.

When I talk to older students about their drawings, what strikes me most is their ability to reflect on their own thinking. Michael, a student in Janet's

FAMILY

HOUSE

Figure 2–4

fifth-grade class, told me how he obtained ideas for his drawing of a 1900 school (Figure 2–4). Like Nicole, he included objects from the artifact centers and added information about children's games and women's work from an oral history interview he had heard during the first week of our explorations. He consciously incorporated this information into his picture. In fact, as he drew, he seemed to engage in ongoing reflection about what made historical sense to him.

Ms. JORGENSEN: We've talked about your school drawing. Where did you get your ideas for other parts of your drawing?

SCHOOL

This is a crowded 1910 class

STREET

FOOD STORE

CHURCH

This downtown street is supposed to be filled with people

Figure 2–4 (continued)

MICHAEL: You know that center where we got all those clothes? I got these (*Points to the dress and the suit on figures in his drawing*) from it. And that (*Points to a pipe in the male figure's mouth*), too. And the lady stays at home. That's why I put the pot in it. And these (*Points to the children*) play marbles.

MS. JORGENSEN: Where did you get the idea about the marbles?

MICHAEL: From the lady's story [a taped oral history at one of the centers]. The kids played that.

MS. JORGENSEN: What about the house?

MICHAEL: I thought the houses would be small but that's, like, a guess. I put the tall grass because, maybe—I didn't know if they'd invented a lawn mower then. That's why there's tall grass.

MS. JORGENSEN: What about your street scene?

MICHAEL: I put a church, food store, and other stores. There would have been other stores and, like, there would have been a lot of people and a bar and people. I put some houses.

MS. JORGENSEN: Where did you get those ideas?

MICHAEL: Some of them, like the houses, I got from movies. I guess movies from the 1900s. Then from some picture I saw there was a bar and, like, stores and people. I drew a picture of a lot of people walking, maybe to the store. Maybe because there weren't any cars at all, so I replaced the cars with people. I got the idea of the stores, maybe from a movie, an old-fashioned movie from 1900.

MS. JORGENSEN: Do you remember which movie?

MICHAEL: No. There's a lot of them.

At one point in his drawing, Michael showed that he could extrapolate an idea using historical reasoning. When I asked him to tell me how he came up with his downtown street scene, he said that he made a picture of "lots of people walking" because he reasoned that "because there weren't any cars at all" he could "replace the cars with people." Unlike Kathy and Nicole, Michael was clearly aware that some of these ideas came from "movies from the 1900s."

Michael's comments illustrate an important point about the teaching value of history drawings. By asking him to draw the inside of a turn-of-the-century school, I encouraged him to put his isolated hypotheses about schooling into a context. As he drew, he searched his memory for images and ideas to synthesize into a picture of an old-fashioned schoolroom. He made dozens of small decisions as he worked, aware that these decisions had to make historical sense. My questions helped him understand the origin of his visual impressions and ideas. For Michael, Kathy, and Nicole, drawing provided a context for linking predictions together and for rethinking their historical meaning. For Kathy, in particular, drawing provided time for reflection, time for discovering the fragments of a future story.

COMPARING MILIEU DRAWINGS

If I run more than one history workshop during the year, I try to find time to ask children to compare their milieu drawings. I do this because I want them to see relationships between historical peoples and to connect these milieus to the sweep of history. After all, history is the study of continuity and change over time, and I want children to see this in a concrete way.

I usually start our conferences by asking students to think about which milieu precedes the other in time. I was able to ask students this question in James's room because when we finished the Ohlone stories we conducted a second workshop focusing on turn-of-the-century Alameda. For a week students explored the new centers we had set up and then drew the 1900 milieu showing a school interior, a street scene, a family, and a house. We talked to them as they drew and later asked them to compare the turn-of-the-century and the Ohlone milieus.

I spoke with Tanya first. She had discarded her first attempt at an Ohlone drawing after looking around the table and discovering that other students were making tepees while she was busy creating a little square house with flowers and a rainbow. Tanya frequently misconstrued directions, but this time I thought she had initially been unsure what the Ohlone milieu looked like. Her revised Ohlone drawing is shown in Figure 2–5. When I asked her to compare her Ohlone drawing with her turn-of-the-century drawing (Figure 2–6), Tanya had difficulty relating the two milieus in time and space. As I talked with Tanya, I realized that even though she wrote an Ohlone piece that made fairly good historical sense, she just wasn't ready to put what we had studied into a wider perspective.

Ms. JORGENSEN: Which of the people that you drew came first in time, the Ohlones or the Alamedians at the turn of the century?
TANYA: The Alamedians came first.
Ms. JORGENSEN: How do you know that?
TANYA: They were about 1850 or something, 1900. The Ohlones, I don't know about them.
Ms. JORGENSEN: So how do you know that the people who lived in Alameda in 1900 came first?
TANYA: I don't know about the Ohlones. Well, these people (*Points to 1900 drawing*) came around 1800, the Victorians, and they started moving into houses. Because they had nice houses that had attics. The mom and dad could have an office and the kids could play games.
Ms. JORGENSEN: Do you think the Victorians that you drew were alive when the Ohlones came along?
TANYA: Yes.
Ms. JORGENSEN: How do you know that?
TANYA: I don't know.
Ms. JORGENSEN: What did other places in the world look like during Ohlone times?
TANYA: Other parts they were doing business, working, having fun, going places with their sons and daughters.
Ms. JORGENSEN: What did it look like?
TANYA: It looked like today.

Figure 2–5

MS. JORGENSEN: What about during this time, the turn of the century, what did it look like in other places then?
TANYA: (*Long pause, shrugs shoulders*)

James wanted to talk to Bradley. We had discussed Bradley's growth on several occasions as we drove home from school in the spring. Bradley was in my reading program in second grade and had a reputation for behavior problems. He did well in James's room, however, and seemed to thrive

Figure 2–5 (continued)

during the Ohlone workshop. One day in May, James pulled him aside and asked him about his Ohlone and turn-of-the-century drawings (Figures 2–7 and 2–8).

Mr. Venable: Do you think the people in your Ohlone drawing knew about the people you drew in your turn-of-the-century drawing?

Bradley: (*Long pause*) Yeah, because they were here longer than the people at the turn of the century.

Mr. Venable: How do you know that?

Figure 2–6

BRADLEY: (*Long pause*) I don't know.

MR. VENABLE: Did the people in your 1900 drawing know about the Ohlones?

BRADLEY: Probably. (*Long pause*) They probably—they [Ohlones] don't go into their [1900] territory, but they [1900] go into theirs [Ohlones]. These people [1900] probably went by their [Ohlones'] camp and they [1900] saw them [Ohlones].

Figure 2–6 (continued)

Bradley had a hard time responding to James's questions. I'm sure he had never thought about them before, and he wasn't used to talking nondefensively to teachers. What little he did articulate indicated that he believed that the two milieus, turn-of-the-century urban Alameda and the Bayside Ohlone villages of the fifteenth century, existed virtually side by side in time and space. This was striking because we had spent time talking about how long ago the Ohlones lived in Alameda. Our talking obviously hadn't affected

Figure 2–7

Bradley's thinking. Perhaps in his mind, an urban Alamedian could simply ride out of town and go "by their camp" and see them. This sounded to me like a John Wayne Western, where Indians and settlers contacted each other but lived in "their own territory." It seemed as if Bradley had chunked the two settings together into a large, undifferentiated milieu modeled after images he'd seen on TV and in the movies. A number of James's third graders linked their drawings in a similar way.

Figure 2–7 (continued)

Joan's understanding of how the milieus in her drawings (Figures 2–9 and 2–10) fit into the broader sweep of history was much more complex than either Bradley's or Tanya's. During Joan's conversation with James, she exhibited the same flexible thinking I witnessed when I talked to her about her earthquake and Santa Cruz stories. Joan clearly had a theory about how the Ohlones and the turn-of-the-century Alamedians were related to each other.

Figure 2–8

MR. VENABLE: Which milieu of time came first, the Ohlones or the
   Victorians?
JOAN: The Ohlones.
MR. VENABLE: How do you know that?
JOAN: Well, I don't think that they would just build things and everything
   and just take it down. They wouldn't have all that stuff built up and then
   just tear it down so (*Laughs*) so that some other people could make
   their own scene and then they would just have to build it back again. If

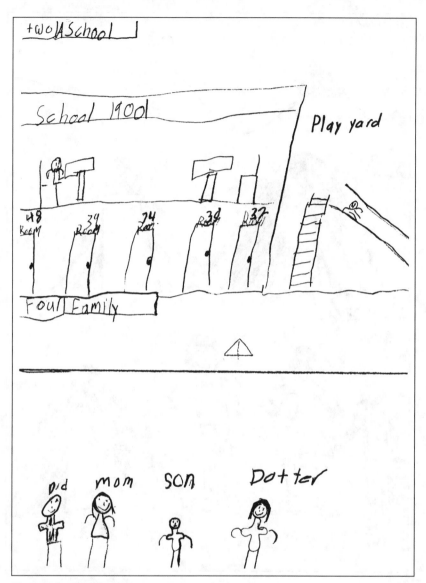

Figure 2–8 (continued)

they made it that way they wouldn't just tear it down and then build it back the way it was just because some people wanted to live outside.

MR. VENABLE: Do you think the Victorians knew about the Ohlones?

JOAN: Yes, they probably had to know about them.

MR. VENABLE: How do you think they found out about them?

JOAN: Maybe, like, they found signs of them. Maybe when they got there they would see some of the homes left, if they got there earlier. They might have seen what the houses looked like and maybe some of the

Figure 2–9

     people. Maybe some of the Ohlones stayed, well, maybe for a while and then they found out that they couldn't do things like they wanted and they didn't want to do all the rules and then they wanted to go away.

MR. VENABLE: Was there a period of time between the time the Ohlones lived in Alameda and the time the people in your 1900 drawing lived?

JOAN: Maybe.

MR. VENABLE: Do you have any idea what it was like?

Figure 2–9 (continued)

JOAN: Like it was probably quiet and there might have been a problem like a water drought or something and there were only a few people there and the other people went somewhere else and the turn-of-the-century people saw that the land was empty and they probably just made it look like this (*Points to 1900 drawing*).

While Bradley saw the milieus linked together like settlers and Indians in a Western movie, Joan theorized that the two cultures somewhat overlapped,

Figure 2–10

with the Ohlones gradually leaving the area and the more modern culture taking over "when the land was empty."

Our interviews with Tanya, Bradley, and Joan illustrate how assessment and teaching in the workshop go hand in hand. As students pose questions about what they want to know, they think about what they already believe. As we probe to find out more about what they know, we stimulate them to rethink and clarify their ideas. The questioning-rethinking process never ends. I'm fairly certain that Tanya and Bradley and Joan never pondered

Figure 2–10 (continued)

questions like ours before. No doubt this was the first time anyone had asked them to try to put together this complex historical puzzle. And that was part of our purpose.

Renegotiating at the Centers

$\mathbf{A}$fter they have explored the artifacts displayed in the centers and drawn pictures of the historical milieu, I ask students to return to the centers to look at new firsthand sources. I change my history talk at this point, hoping to stimulate students to rethink their ideas and in this way to renegotiate the meaning of the artifacts. When students make a prediction or ask for my opinion, I offer my ideas and encourage them to critically examine their own.

For the Native American workshop in James's classroom, I borrowed museum photographs and artists' drawings depicting Ohlone life and distributed them among the history centers. James asked his students to pay special attention to images that surprised them, especially things that were different from their own drawings. We circulated from center to center, talking with small groups of students and listening to their comments. A tape recorder picked up this conversation between Nicole, Thomas, and Ben, who were discussing a photograph of a woman pounding acorns with a mortar and pestle. The "brush" they refer to was lying on a straw mat next to an Ohlone cooking basket.

BEN: Now we know! She used, like, one of those chopper things.
NICOLE: She used those to chop it, to make it.
THOMAS: The brush!
NICOLE: Look at the brush.
BEN: I know. They used that for hair. Just brush it back, I guess.
THOMAS: And they're using that smasher . . .
NICOLE: . . . to make food and smashing . . .
THOMAS: They must be crushing nuts. They must be crushing nuts.

These students were excited, and so were the other students at the various centers around the room. They spent several weeks predicting how the Ohlone artifacts were made and used, and they drew villages and Ohlone families, searching their memories for images that made sense to them. They used the photographs and drawings to confirm these predictions, and many of them were ecstatic, believing that they had finally solved an important mystery. As Ben said, "Now we know!"

As I move from center to center, I model historical thinking and pose questions to stimulate further insights. This is an important part of the process of revising earlier ideas. When James joined Nicole, Ben, and Thomas a few minutes after Ben's "Now we know!" he helped the three clarify their ideas about how the Ohlones cooked in straw baskets. James asked them to tell him what they noticed. Thomas believed that the cooking in the photograph was different from the cooking described in *The Adventures of Little Bird*. James asked Thomas to describe the difference, and by showing them a way to think about the details in the photograph, he helped the group predict how the cooking rocks were used.

MR. VENABLE: What have you noticed?

THOMAS: It's different, like in cooking, like they said in *Little Bird*.

MR. VENABLE: What's different about it?

THOMAS: (*Referring to a special pair of sticks used to get hot cooking rocks from the fire to the basket*) They're using a "clipper" to pick it up?

MR. VENABLE: I don't remember if they described that part in *Little Bird*. What do you think they are going to do with that stone?

NICOLE: Putting it in the fire?

MR. VENABLE: Could be, or maybe putting it into . . .

BEN: The basket?

MR. VENABLE: That makes sense. Why are they putting it in the basket?

NICOLE: They put it in before they put the food in.

MR. VENABLE: Why would they do that?

BEN: To clean it?

MR. VENABLE: Do you think they put it in hot or cold?

BEN: I don't know.

MR. VENABLE: I'm wondering about the fire in this photograph. I'm thinking that they might have used the fire to heat up the rock. What do you think?

NICOLE: I know. They cooked it, because the rock was hot. They cooked the acorns after the hot rock got put into the basket. It cooked it up.

The children studied the photographs for another day, and then we put out books and articles about the artifacts, seeds, shells, and native plants. The new resources allowed us to focus negotiations further, this time by modeling how to use printed information to discover how artifacts functioned.

MR. VENABLE: I see you're playing the gambling game.

RICO: Yes, but we don't know how you win.

MR. VENABLE: Here, we can read about it. That last sentence tells you how to tally the score. Read it out loud for us and let's listen closely.

PETE: (*Reading*) "If all flat or rounded sides turn up, it's two points. If an equal number of flat or rounded sides come up, it's one point."

MR. VENABLE: So what does that tell us?

PETE: If you get all the round sides, you get two points, and if you get three round sides, you get one point.

MR. VENABLE: Is that all?

RICO: And it's the same for the flats.

MR. VENABLE: Makes sense to me. Does anyone remember who can play this game?

PETE: I think that the men can play the women and the women can play the women, but the men can't play the men.

MR. VENABLE: That's what I think, too. Okay, let's get the game and play it.

During this phase of the workshop I initiate other kinds of negotiations. Sometimes I demonstrate how an object works. A good example of this occurred in Janet's room when Jose and I helped Michael and Booker learn to operate a 1910 meat grinder at the kitchen gadget center.

BOOKER: I think this is a meat grinder. Do you put the meat in here?

MS. JORGENSEN: Good question. Does anyone know how the meat grinder works?

JOSE: I do. I think I know. My aunt has one kind of like this. You put it on a table. (*Jose holds up the grinder; Ms. Jorgensen assists*) Then you put a small plate or bowl right here and grind it. It all falls down.

MS. JORGENSEN: Where do you put the meat in?

JOSE: Down here.

MS. JORGENSEN: That makes sense. They pushed the meat down with their hands or a wooden spoon or something, and pushed it real hard. And it comes out here.

BOOKER: (*Holds up another grinding plate for the nose of the grinder*) And this makes it smaller.

MS. JORGENSEN: Good, and you can make it coarser or finer by changing that. Do you see people using this today?

JOSE: My aunt does. She just got a new one.

BOOKER: We don't have one.

MS. JORGENSEN: People had these more often in 1900. Why do you think they had them?

BOOKER: Maybe the store didn't grind it up?

MS. JORGENSEN: That's a good guess. They had small butcher shops in those days. Also, women did a lot more cooking at home and they had to process a lot of their own food, like grinding up meat and making their own jam.

As I walk from center to center, I also demonstrate how to "read" photographs and written sources. In Janet's class Ali was exploring a schoolbook. Like many of his peers, his initial observations were superficial. I wanted to help him look more carefully and think about what he saw.

MS. JORGENSEN: Ali, what have you noticed?

ALI: I'm looking at the word list that tells you how the words are spelled.

MS. JORGENSEN: Oh, what kind of a book is that?

ALI: I saw a poem in here, and I saw some stories.

MS. JORGENSEN: What does that tell you?

ALI: Maybe they read it at home?

MS. JORGENSEN: Do you think kids or adults read this book?

ALI: I think it was for kids because I see some easy words, and I don't think grown-ups would be interested in the stories.

MS. JORGENSEN: You're using good reasoning. That makes sense to me. What can you tell by reading the title?

ALI: It says *The McGuffey Reader Book Five.*

MS. JORGENSEN: What does that tell you?

ALI: That it was a grade book?

MS. JORGENSEN: What do you mean, "grade book"?

ALI: Like a fifth-grade book?

MS. JORGENSEN: Good guess. So what kind of a book is this?

ALI: Maybe a book that kids used at school.

MS. JORGENSEN: Makes sense. Have you read any of it?

ALI: Yeah, I read a little bit of a poem and looked at the words.

MS. JORGENSEN: How does it compare to the books you read in here?

ALI: Well, there's no color in it. And the words are funny. Kids had to read good in those days. This poem, the one on this page? It's really hard.

MS. JORGENSEN: What kind of a schoolbook is this?

ALI: For spelling?

MS. JORGENSEN: I think that it was used for that. But I'm wondering whether it wasn't also used to teach reading because it has stories and poems, and it's called a "reader." Why don't you read more and see what else you can find out.

My questions are invitations, enticements for further inquiry. Without them, Ali might have moved on, gaining less from the experience.

At the beginning of most workshops I teach a formal minilesson. In these whole-group demonstrations and discussions I concentrate on how to handle—and obtain information from—the artifacts and other resources in the history centers. I plan these lessons by thinking about the problems and concerns that surface each day. In Janet's class, for instance, I noticed that many students looked quickly through the historical photographs, so I gave a lesson on "reading" photographs. I used a slide of the interior of a 1903 school room and asked students to describe what they saw and compare it with their own classroom. In another lesson, James asked his group to share their predictions about the use of the clapper stick and then examined the artifact itself, modeling how to discover clues to help determine its function.

When the students have had a few weeks to learn about the artifacts displayed at the history centers, I introduce storywriting and continue to read aloud. In our conferences and lessons, we talk about their ideas about the milieu as they struggle to communicate these ideas through written text.

MINILESSONS

I usually give a short minilesson before students start their daily writing. That first year I found that students need help in developing story problems, making historical and people sense, crafting leads and endings, and using historical resources to enrich and extend their pieces. These are complicated writing problems and I know I can't teach children about them in a lockstep way. I need to model how to think about these issues so that students can think about them on their own.

Early in the first week of writing I "think out loud" about possible story problems. On the first day in Janet's fifth-grade classroom, I talked about my ideas for a story set at the turn of the century to demonstrate my thinking. I wanted students to be aware of some of the issues I weighed as I thought about what to write:

> You know, I've been thinking about what I want to write. I have a couple of ideas and I wanted to think out loud about them with you today. Now I know I have a lot of choices. I could write about a big event, like, I thought about the 1906 earthquake in San Francisco. That was really devastating. I could imagine writing a story about a family going through the earthquake and then trying to survive in the city, maybe coming over here to Alameda because their house burns down. I could write that. In some ways, I can imagine this story and how a family might have felt. We've been through a pretty bad earthquake recently. That makes this idea more real to me, helps me imagine how the story might go.
>
> I also thought of another story idea last night. This one really appeals to me, and I'm not sure why. I was thinking I could write about how girls couldn't wear pants in 1900 and what kinds of problems this might create for them. Now that I think about it, I think this story idea appeals to me because in the forties when I was about your age, it was sort of okay for girls to wear pants, but I mostly wore skirts and dresses to school. I remember how hard it was to climb on the monkey bars and play sometimes with a skirt on. So I guess I know a little bit about how it might have felt in the early 1900s when girls didn't have any choices. Now what kind of a problem can I make out of that idea? I could have a really sassy character in my story—a little girl who likes to break the rules, who maybe likes to play rough games and ride bikes. As I'm thinking about it, I would have to have a character like that in order to have my story make sense. Regular girls back then wouldn't have cared about wearing pants. Okay, so I have this sassy little girl, and maybe I get her to steal her brother's knickers so that she can ride a bike. Yes, I like that idea. I think that would make a good story problem.

Later in the workshop, I show students how I use firsthand sources and resource books to make my story more historical. During the second week of writing with Janet's fifth graders, I talked to the class about the trouble I was having visualizing the brother's knickers. At one point I walked over to one of the centers, picked up a historical photograph, and described the clothing in the picture. "How disappointing," I said. "The little boy in the photograph is wearing long pants." I wondered out loud whether kids really wore knickers in 1900. Then I picked up a facsimile reprint of the *Bloomingdale's Illustrated 1886 Catalog* and commented on it as I browsed through pages of dry goods, housewares, and fashions. I stopped on page 104 and read an ad for the New Brunswick suit "for dress, made in the most stylish manner and of the best materials, suitable for a boy four to thirteen years of age, fine imported worsteds, blue-gray and brown." "What a find," I remarked. Not only did the advertisement provide a lithograph of a boy wearing knickers, I found other information that I could use in my story. I could say the pants were made out of worsted wool and I knew they could be gray or brown.

Many of the writing lessons explore whether a story makes historical sense. James discussed this issue with his students when he shared his piece about a boy who worried that he'd fail on his first hunt. James brought his story to the group and asked them to identify the "Ohloneness" in his writing.

MR. VENABLE: I wrote some more on my story last night and I'd like to read it to you and then have you help me by telling me the parts of my story that make Ohlone sense to you. (*Reads story*) I think that putting in that he had to fast before the hunt made good historical sense. What else?

VEUN: The part where Deerwatcher wanted to hunt the deer and Deerwatcher went to the woods and had a dream and the dream was true. The deer was really on the outside.

MR. VENABLE: Yes, I think so, too.

JIMMY: Because he had to dream of deer so he could hunt.

CHRISTINA: There were traders from another village.

BRADLEY: Trees.

MR. VENABLE: How do the trees make historical sense in my story?

CARL: 'Cause they lived outside a lot.

MR. VENABLE: You mean that there were lots of trees and hills and grass and no big buildings during Ohlone times? Yes, that makes sense. What else?

CARL: They were in a tule boat.

MR. VENABLE: Yes, I didn't put them in a motor boat. The Ohlones had boats made out of tule grass, so this made sense, too.

James told the group that he thought the "fast" in his story made historical sense. Carl, Christina, Veun, Jimmy, and Bradley pointed out other parts of the story that made it sound authentic. But some students were confused. It was difficult for them to understand how the milieu in the story was different from modern Alameda. Because this is a difficult concept for young children, I often repeat historical-sense lessons throughout the course of the workshop.

Sometimes I use minilessons to address specific confusions or problems. At one point James noticed that only a few of the children's stories made reference to the importance of water in Ohlone culture. The Ohlones were shellgatherers, people who built villages next to the rivers that lead to the Bay. He decided that he wanted to talk about this one more time, hoping to get some of his student writers to incorporate this information into their stories. His lesson was very simple. He read a short excerpt from *The Ohlone Way,* lead a brief discussion, and asked students to think of ways to use this information to refine the setting for their stories.

CONFERRING

The conference is the heart of my interaction with students. In these student/teacher transactions, I often reinforce what I have discussed during minilessons. It took us months to refine this dialogue, and in many ways, I think it was the hardest part of our job. James and I weren't satisfied with our conferences the first year. We knew that they were a critical component of the workshop, but in September we weren't sure how to use them sensitively and effectively.

I think we overreacted that first year, misunderstanding our role as elders and underplaying our ideas in an attempt to establish a balance of power between ourselves and our students. I remember one particular conference, with Judy. She was writing a mystery and insisted that people drove cars in San Francisco during the 1850 gold rush. As I listened to her, I wasn't sure how to respond. Should I say, "No, Judy, you are wrong. I know that cars were invented later in the century." Would I own too much of her story if I said this and questioned her historical understanding? And what about the kids whose stories were filled with other unexpected responses? Was there enough time to talk with them about each issue? Was it all right not to talk about all of these issues? Would too much questioning discourage them from writing? During the Ohlone workshop, James and I worked at refining how we talked with students and on clarifying our role in student/teacher transactions. I conferred with his students, and I also worked with Janet's fifth graders. As we interacted with the children we monitored our history talk and learned to negotiate in a variety of ways.

In the conferences on historical sense, I want students to examine their responses and refine their understanding of historical materials. I use a number of questions to stimulate rethinking as we talk about their writing.

How do we know that your story takes place in 1900?
Is there anything in your story that you think might not have happened during these times?

What makes historical sense in your piece?

What doesn't make historical sense in your piece?

How do the actions of your characters tell us that this story is a Victorian story?

Does that make turn-of-the-century sense to you?

How do you think the Victorians would have felt about that?

What would someone living in 1900 have done in that situation?

I know that your story is published and that you are not going to revise it anymore, but I wanted you to think about it for a minute. Is there anything in your story that you think might not make historical sense?

I ask questions like these throughout the workshop, although sometimes I don't ask them right away. During the second week of writing in Janet's class, I talked to Sophia for the first time about the historical content of her piece. She had used historical resources to research information on home remedies to add to her story. Her piece was complicated, and I wasn't surprised that she was slightly off on some subtle details. I wanted to talk to her about one of these details—the use of the word "blocks"—which, in the context of her writing, was an anachronism. Similar unexpected responses surfaced in most workshop stories, although they were more common in the third grade.

MS. JORGENSEN: You've worked very hard on your story. I noticed the part at the beginning where you describe how the mom makes a home remedy. I can really picture it—you say she squeezed the water out of the rag and rubbed it in the bowl with the ground root. This part really makes your story seem like it takes place in 1900. What else in your story makes historical sense?

SOPHIA: The old village, the girl's dress, not being able to call the doctor on the phone.

MS. JORGENSEN: Yes, that makes 1900 sense to me. There's another part in your piece that I wanted to talk to you about. You say that "the doctor lived a few blocks away." Then you call this place a "village." I'm wondering what this village looks like?

SOPHIA: It's in the middle of some hills, and over here (*Gestures with her hand*) is a couple of houses—like rows of houses. There's no one in this part.

MS. JORGENSEN: You say "rows of houses"? Are there lots of houses?

SOPHIA: No, just a few.

MS. JORGENSEN: What do the houses look like?

SOPHIA: They're sort of bungalows, small houses, old houses.

MS. JORGENSEN: So your village sounds small, like there aren't too many houses. I'm wondering about the word "blocks." When I hear people use the word "blocks" it makes me think of a pretty modern city or even a town around the turn of the century, but a big town with streets and lots of houses.

SOPHIA: Maybe I could say, "a few houses away."

MS. JORGENSEN: Yes, or "a couple of houses away." That would make better historical sense. It also might help the reader if you describe what the village looks like, like you just did for me.

I also confer with students about writing fiction. Fiction was difficult for James's third graders and a challenge for the students in Janet's fifth-grade class. It was hard for both groups to define story problems, develop characters, and create logical links between events. In these conferences, I talk about how to make "people sense" in a story by asking:

What is the story problem in your piece?
Do the characters in your story have a problem to solve?
Does this problem make "people sense"?
What are your characters going to do to solve this problem?
Does it make sense that your character did that?
Do people act that way?
What do you think someone would do next?
You told me what your character did. What is she going to do next?
What's going to happen next?
Do your characters have names?
I am having a hard time telling your characters apart. Could you tell me more about them? How are they related to each other?
Why do you think your character did that?
Why is your character going to do that?
Is this character important to your story?
Why is this character important to your story?

James spent a lot of time exploring "people sense" with his third graders. He talked to Billy about his story on the fourth day of writing. Billy's piece was about an Ohlone boy who got lost in the forest and was attacked by a man from a nearby village.

MR. VENABLE: Let me see if I can retell your story. It's about a boy named Running Fox who goes into the forest to hunt and he gets lost. A man from a village sneaks up on him and tries to hurt him. The boy fights back and kills the man. Then the father comes and tells the boy to come home. Is that pretty much what your story is about?
BILLY: Yes, and he throws stones at him.
MR. VENABLE: There's a part in your story that doesn't make people sense to me. You say that Running Fox's father comes and says that it's time to come home to eat. Do you think that's what the father would say when he first sees him after he's been lost for so long?
BILLY: Maybe he's surprised to see him? I think I could put, like the boy was hungry and then he says, "I killed the bad man!" and his father says, "What?"
MR. VENABLE: That makes more sense to me. How does the father find him?

BILLY: He could follow a trail and find him.

MR. VENABLE: Okay, you need to think about those parts of your story. Think about how you can make those parts make more sense.

James had a number of concerns about Billy's piece, but in this conference he directed Billy's attention to two parts of his story that didn't make sense. Running Fox's father was a flat, undeveloped character who responded to seeing his long-lost son by telling him that it was time for dinner. James questioned whether this made sense, trying to get Billy to examine his character's motivations. How did the father find his son? Billy didn't tell us, and James thought that it was important for him to provide a logical link between these events.

I also ask process questions about writing and thinking when I confer with students. Although these questions are important, I probably don't ask them often enough. In conferences I try to create an open-ended dialogue beginning with "What do you think about your story?" "Where did you get your ideas for your drawing?" or "How did you come to that conclusion?" I also ask students to identify artifacts, photographs, books, and articles they have used in their drawing or writing. I pose these questions to assess their understanding and to stimulate self-evaluation and reflection. In many ways, these conferences are similar to the process conferences I conduct in writing workshop when I ask students to tell me how they solve specific writing problems, encouraging them to define their audience and evaluate their work.

CREATING SHARED UNDERSTANDINGS

I type final drafts and publish student writing in individual books and/or in a magazine that focuses on the milieu. In whole-group meetings I help children celebrate what we've learned and map the content of their collected works by discussing the connections between the stories. I want children to understand that each piece reflects the writer's unique experiences and ideas yet contributes to the group's shared understanding of the past.

In James's class, we produced a magazine about the Ohlone people. The children brainstormed about selection criteria and listed the qualities they expected to see in a good story or informational piece. Then they selected an editorial committee of three students who reviewed the stories submitted by other writers in the class. James typed the selected stories and the students illustrated the magazine. The group discussed how the collection represented a special view of Ohlone life, with stories about hunting, food gathering, sickness, death, native games, and medicines.

I also wanted Janet's fifth graders to see that their individual stories were pieces to a puzzle, each piece telling us something about urban areas in the United States in 1900. I did this by holding special author celebrations in which writers read their finished work and the class acknowledged the work by retelling parts of the story that made historical sense. I mapped this information on a sheet of paper under the title "U.S. City Life in 1900" (Figure 2–11).

NATURAL DISASTERS

1906 San Francisco earthquake was destructive
-Fazel, Sophia, David, & Dorothy

IMMIGRATION

People came from China
-Michael

FAMILY LIFE

Washed clothes by hand, etc.
-Tanisha

Celebrated Christmas differently
-Booker

RACE RELATIONS

People discriminated against Blacks
-Keith

CRIME

Kids got kidnapped
-David

U.S.
City Life
in
1900

ILLNESS/MEDICINE

People made medicine at home
-Sue & Mary

People died of small pox
-Albert

SCHOOL

Some schools had one room, etc.
-Sue, Tommy Christopher, & Juanita

CLOTHING STYLES

Girls couldn't wear pants
-Gloria, Elizabeth, & Abbey

INVENTIONS

Telephones made it easy to talk
-Jose

LEISURE

Families went on picnics
-Ali

Kids played baseball
-Ian

Kids collected tobacco cards
-Terry & John

Kids rode bikes
-Gloria

Kids played marbles and jacks
-Noralyn & Booker

Cars were cheap
-Allen

The Titanic sunk
-Mostafa

Figure 2–11

Our shared understanding of each historical milieu was unique to each class. I wouldn't expect another group of third graders to create the same Ohlone magazine, nor would the composite view of life in 1900 be the same in another fifth grade down the hall from Janet's classroom. The past as reconstructed by one class is never the same as the past as reconstructed by another. The writers are different, their viewpoints are different, and their sense of history is different.

The history that emerged in the two classrooms after weeks of reading, writing, drawing, talking, and thinking wasn't identical to the history embedded in the adopted third- and fifth-grade textbooks or in district or state guidelines. We focused on limited aspects of social history with both groups because that's what interested our students. The history the students encountered in the workshop was fragmented and incomplete in the same way that knowledge is fragmented and incomplete in the writing workshop. Yet because as a writing teacher I trust that over the long haul students will realize their full potential as writers, as a history teacher I also trust that youngsters will eventually expand their interests to include political and economic history, will develop their own understanding of the past, and will realize their full potential as historians.

PART THREE

Children Reconstructing the Past:
Case Studies
· · · · · · · · · · · · · · · · · ·

Case studies provide an in-depth view of the complex processes children go through as they struggle to clarify and communicate historical meaning. In looking at the experiences of individual students, I learn something new about language acquisition and deepen my appreciation of children's understanding of the past.

This section looks closely at four students: Sandra, Elizabeth, Tanisha, and Veun. In some ways they represent an ethnic and social cross-section of the children at Washington School. Sandra, age eight, and Elizabeth, age ten, both Caucasian, are identified as "gifted and talented," although Elizabeth is also in special education because

· ·

she has a "learning disability." Tanisha, age ten, is African American, is in fifth grade, and qualifies for the Title I reading program. Veun is in third grade, speaks Vietnamese, and receives extra help several times a week in the English as a second language program.

I am fascinated by these students' conversations, drawings, and writings about history. As I worked with them, I grew to appreciate their individual ways of using language to describe and understand the world. Their stories provide insights into a number of perplexing and important problems related to writing about and thinking about history.

• •

Sandra

Sandra was a bright, cocky eight-year-old. Her "Well, what do *you* have to offer?" attitude was one of the first things I noticed about her. And I'm not sure whether it was the way she walked into James's classroom with her blond hair carelessly bouncing up and down or that little "Aren't I cute and smart?" tone in her voice that told me how aware she was that she was an academically talented if not gifted child. It took me a while to see the shy little girl in her, the little girl who wanted so much to please her teachers and parents and sometimes felt separate from her peers.

In October, Sandra chose to read Elizabeth Coerr's *Sadako and a Thousand Paper Cranes* with Pete, Carl, Rico, Tim, and Billy. She was a quiet contributor to the group, and I wondered if she deferred to the boys during their discussions because she was the only girl. I saw Sandra talk a great deal in other settings, often dominating the conversation, so I decided that I would encourage her to speak at the first opportunity. That opportunity came a few days after the group read the third chapter of *Sadako*. During a quiet time in the room, I asked the six of them what they thought Alameda looked like about the time Sadako was alive. Carl said that Alameda probably "looked like *Little House in the Big Woods.*" Sandra didn't respond right away, but I could tell by the way she wiggled in her chair that she disagreed with him. I finally asked her, because I wondered what she was thinking. After a short silence she told us that it couldn't have looked that way "because there weren't a lot of clues in the book like that. And they had parks and stuff in the story."

That's all Sandra said that day, but her words told me she had a clear sense that *Sadako* took place in modern times. She wrote a succinct summary of the theme of the story in her history response log, and she showed no confusion when she again described the setting to me a day later. When she finished *Sadako*, Sandra went on to read Clyde Bulla's *A Lion to Guard Us* independently but later chose not to read another historical book from the library.

Sandra had an unusual ability to think abstractly, and I wondered what she already knew about Native American life. Was the milieu in her mind filled with bows and arrows, tepees, war paint, and feathered Indians? I was eager to read her history response log entries for the first week of the workshop. I wondered what she knew and what she wanted to know about the Ohlones. This is what she wrote:

> If I were to stand in Alameda when there were only Native Americans here, I think I would see lots of trees. I would see different kinds of houses. You would see Indians with bows and arrows. If it were in the winter, the houses would keep out rain, sleet, hail, and snow.
>
> The Ohlones mostly had black hair. They wore bear skin. They had different shades of eyes. They helped their parents. They were nice to other

people. They liked to fish. They picked berries. They killed deer. They caught fish for food and picked berries. They picked plants, too.

Later in her log, she describes what she thinks the Ohlones did when they were not hunting or gathering. According to Sandra, the Ohlones "played with their kids. They rested, made music. They did some writing. They did some errands. They read from books, and they slept."

Despite the presence of books, writing, and "errands," Sandra's depiction of the milieu was amazingly accurate. When I read her log, I was struck by the number of expected responses. The Ohlones picked berries and plants, wore bearskins, liked to fish, played with their children, and were nice to other people. Sandra's depiction also impressed me because it was devoid of the usual violent TV stereotypes. She seemed to see the Ohlones as the gentle, caring people most historians believe they were. When I asked her how she knew all this, she told me, "It comes from my head. It's all from my imagination." I wasn't surprised by this. Even though she was very bright, Sandra, like other third graders, couldn't tell me where she got her ideas.

On the first day of the students' artifact exploration, Sandra chose to go to the center with the gambling game and the doll. She made a number of predictions there, including her guess that the clapper stick was a "flute." On the second day her group rotated to the listening center and heard a story about hunting and another about taking care of Ohlone babies. Sandra remarked in her log that she thought that some of what she heard was "weird."

On the third day, Sandra came to life. I observed her across the room with Margaret, Kathy, and Joan at the animal-skin center. Their conversation was very animated. In fact, at several points Sandra and Joan took turns draping themselves with skins and role-playing that they were animals chasing one another. Sandra wrote in her log:

> I had on a fox fur. I pretended that I was a fierce fox. I practically scared everyone. I noticed some interesting fur. Some of it was soft and some of it was rough. Did they cut off the head? I hope so. I think if I cut the head it would be pretty disgusting. What did they use the fur for? Clothing? I don't know. I hope to find out the answer.

Sandra's entry confirmed my observations. She spent part of her time at the center engaged in imaginative dialogue with Nancy. She described this role-playing as "pretend[ing] that I was a fierce fox." She went on to discuss the furs more analytically, predicting at one point that they were used for clothing. She thought about what it meant to prepare the skins and stated that if she had to "cut the head, it would be pretty disgusting." The next day, Sandra reported a similar mix of role-playing and analysis at two other centers. She wrote:

> I pretended that I was weaving a basket. I noticed that there were arrowheads. I guessed that these funny-looking things were to hold food over the fire. There was a gadget to drill holes. I wondered if those things were bones. And if they were, who would it come from. There was a top. It was made out

of acorns with a thing sticking out of it. I saw a bowl made out of stone with a big stone in it. You put acorns in it and make acorn mush. I liked the top. I spun it. It twirled.

It was breakfast time. Who wants the coffee? Here's the waffle. Well, let's get back to reality. There were clam shells. I thought that the shells over by the acorns were beautiful. There were green plants that I watered yesterday. They were coming up fine. Seeds were in a bag. We used them for coffee beans. They spilled while I was writing this. There were buckeyes. I thought that the shells were pretty. I thought that if it were breakfast, I'd hate it!

Sandra's entries struck me because they contained so few unexpected responses. And like Christina and her peers (page 40), she continually made predictions: the sticks were for putting food on the fire, the acorn was a top, the plants and shells were Ohlone food. She engaged in role-playing at the centers, using the artifacts as props. Sometimes her minidramas had nothing to do with the Ohlones: the seeds at one point were a convenient prop for making coffee. At other times, she seemed to be using the artifacts to help her imagine what it was like to live in Ohlone times, weaving baskets and preparing a shellfish meal.

After observing Sandra at the artifact centers, I anticipated that her history drawing would contain very few unexpected responses. As I watched from across the room on the first day of drawing, I noticed how intently she worked, not stopping to look around or talk as Tanya and many others did. On the second day, I pulled a chair next to her and sat quietly watching her work. She was aware that I was there and looked at me once out of the corner of eye, never taking her pencil off the paper or breaking her concentration. By now, her drawing of the Ohlone village was complete and she was working on her illustration of "a family busy." (See Figure 3–1.)

I wasn't surprised that Sandra's Ohlone village contained tepees. After all, most children her age watched television and had little other exposure to Native American cultures. Tepees were bound to show up in these drawings. But what about the more gentle image she presented in her response log? I wanted to find out more about the Ohlone milieu she imagined, so I interrupted her work for a few minutes to ask her about her drawing.

Ms. Jorgensen: Tell me about your drawings.
Sandra: Well, they are living in tepees. (*Points to drawing*) They got their fish from the stream here. (*Points to stream in drawing*)
Ms. Jorgensen: Tell me more about the tepees.
Sandra: They put these big things—they are sticks—up, and then they put mud and, like, on them and on the doors.
Ms. Jorgensen: What's going on over here? (*Pointing to the figures at the extreme righthand side of the drawing*)
Sandra: I was thinking that these were guards, up here on the ridge, like if different kinds of Indians come and they want to take stuff, the guard will help.

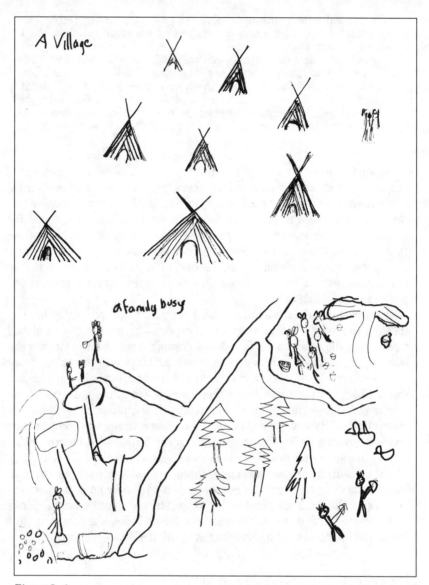

A Village

a family busy

Figure 3–1

Her explanation of the guards surprised me. When I asked her about the apparent contradiction between her original log entries, which portrayed the Ohlones as gentle people, she couldn't explain it. When I reflected on her responses later, it seemed to me that her milieu was a very mixed one in which the Ohlones were gentle at times but capable of violence. Her log gave me part of the picture; her drawing gave me the rest.

I also talked with Sandra about the Ohlone family at the left of her drawing. She had incorporated an image from *The Adventures of Little Bird*

Figure 3–1 (continued)

story that James read two days before. In two places in her picture, she drew Ohlones gathering acorns with a basket. She said she didn't know about acorn gathering before Mr. Venable read the story. She also mentioned that a basket and acorns were at one of the centers. I wondered if her sense of the Native American milieu was changing because of the story and the artifacts scattered around the room.

After the second day of drawing, students went back to the centers for more-focused explorations. Sandra chose to go to the listening center again to hear the tape of James telling the Ohlone stories. The next day she went to the plant and shell center with Margaret and Joan. She spent a good deal of her time recording information about a variety of items on the table, sitting on the floor cross-legged in a circle with the other girls and occasionally going back to the table to examine a container of seeds or obtain another plant book. She seemed very engaged, recording information about the medicinal and cooking uses of cattails and the woodrose plant.

On the third day, she went to an artifact center containing cooking tools. At one point, she and Tanya got into a long conversation about how people used baskets. They were confused about how the Ohlones heated food in the basket and kept the tule straw from burning. Wouldn't the basket burn if they held it over a fire? Sandra spent several minutes looking for an answer in a book at the center. Before she could find anything, James called the groups to the carpet to listen to another chapter of *Little Bird*. I observed Sandra as James read. When he came to the part of the story where Little Bird's mother cooked acorn mush by putting hot rocks into the water in the basket, Sandra's eyes widened and she looked knowingly across the circle at Tanya. After James finished reading, she raised her hand and said, "We didn't know that they got the hot rocks and put them in it!"

This was a perfect teaching moment. James asked Sandra and Tanya if they wanted to use the basket and the rocks from the center to act out their theory for the class. Sandra walked to the table and picked up the props. As I watched them role-playing, I realized that Sandra had done what we wanted all the students to do: she made a connection between the artifacts and the story. She puzzled over a prediction during free exploration, negotiating with Tanya to try to figure out how the Ohlones used the basket. She heard information in the story that confirmed her prediction and reflected on her experience with the artifacts. We could have told her about the hot rocks, but it wouldn't have meant as much to her as confirming her prediction on her own.

I wondered if any of this—the rocks, the cooking, the plants—would show up in Sandra's writing. When we started our history pieces the following day, she drew a picture (Figure 3–2) and then talked about her story with Joan. She told Joan that she wanted to write a story with chapters, and this is how she started (Sandra's handwritten draft is included at the end of this section as Writing Sample 1):

The Mystery of the House on Philpot Path

Chapter 1: Getting a Shiver
"La, la, de la, la, la," said Starlight, humming to herself. She was picking acorns with her mother. Suddenly a white thing flew toward her! She screamed, and it went away. Her mother turned.
"Why did you scream?" she said, sounding angry.
Starlight looked at her sheepishly. "There was a ghost," she replied.
"Oh," said her mother.

I had a conference with Sandra toward the end of the writing period because I wanted her to identify her story problem and think about what she

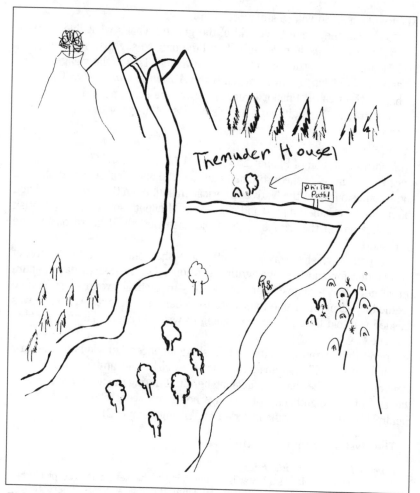

In the drawing: "Themuder House" and "philpot Path!"

Figure 3–2

planned to say next. So far she had written nothing about cooking, but her first attempt to create an Ohlone story showed that she was using her newly revised understanding to recreate the milieu. Acorns and baskets from the artifact center surfaced in her lead sentence. Sandra said the ghost problem was Ohlone because she remembered the dead spirit story from *The Ohlone Way*. I asked her about the characters, and she told me that Starlight was an Ohlone name because it came from nature like the name Little Bird.

MS. JORGENSEN: What's your story about?

SANDRA: It's about a little girl gathering acorns.

MS. JORGENSEN: Do the characters in your story have a problem to solve?

SANDRA: Well, it's about a mystery, about a house on Philpot Hill which ghosts come out of. Haunts people and stuff and the only way to get rid of it is for someone to yell at them.

MS. JORGENSEN: So you're story problem is . . . ?

SANDRA: That they have to get rid of the ghosts. That's what I've written so far. (*Reads the story to me*) Then I'm going to say that something screamed at the little girl. (*Points to drawing*) This is the village, and this is Philpot Path. I got that from *A Lion to Guard Us*. They had a street called Philpot Lane. Anyway, she screams and the mom turns around. Starlight says there's a ghost. I'm going to write more about that.

Sandra's inclusion of Philpot Lane from *A Lion to Guard Us* was curious, since everything else she wrote seemed to make historical sense. It showed some confusion about the Native American milieu, even though she modified the notion by calling it a path and not a lane. "Philpot" sounded very British and unlike any of the names in the Ohlone stories she'd heard during the workshop.

The next day, she worked intently, and she continued almost without interruption for another two writing sessions. On the fourth day, Sandra retold her story—almost word for word—to a small group of girls. She seemed unwilling or unable to deviate from her written text. When she was finished she told them, "Next I'm going to write a chapter about the ghost machine."

I don't think Sandra realized when she announced her plans to the girls that her "machine" was anachronistic. The girls said nothing and Sandra went on to write the chapter, finishing her draft during the next few days. By the end of the eighth day of writing, her story went like this (see also Sandra's handwritten draft, included as Writing Sample 2):

The Mystery of Philpot Path

Chapter 1: Where Is Little Fox?
"La, la, de la, la, la," said Starlight, humming to herself. She was picking acorns with her mother. Suddenly a white thing flew toward her! She screamed and it went away. Her mother turned.

"Why did you scream." she said, sounding angry.

Starlight looked at her sheepishly. "There was a ghost," she replied.

"Oh," said her mother and went back to picking acorns.

When they were walking toward home, Starlight thought, "I will go in that house."

Then they walked in their house. Something was wrong and it only took a second for Starlight to realize what it was! Little Fox, her little brother, was gone!

"Mom, Little Fox is gone," Starlight said.

"He'll be back tonight," her mother said.

Starlight didn't believe her. When night came, Starlight couldn't sleep. She laid awake for a long time.

Chapter 2: The Scream!
The next morning was cold and gray. Starlight woke up. Her mother was making breakfast.

"Did Little Fox come home?" Starlight asked.

"No," her mother said, crying. She wiped her tears and said to Starlight, "Go pick some berries, please." So Starlight went off.

She decided to take a shortcut on Philpot Path. As she approached it, she heard a noise. She came towards it. She heard a long harsh scream that sent a shiver up Starlight's spine. Then she ran away.

Chapter 3: Run Starlight Run

Starlight ran hopelessly, with no idea where she was going. When she stopped, she was lost. Suddenly, she was looking at a face.

"Come here," the lady said, reaching for her. Starlight ducked and ran to the safety of her village.

Chapter 4: The Ghost Machine

When Starlight came home it was six o'clock. Her mother was not angry. That night, Starlight got out of her room and through the door and ran down Philpot Path and ran into the house. As soon as she stepped in, she gasped! There were machines, a dummy, and fake ghosts. Starlight grinned, "So that's where all the ghosts come from," she thought.

She saw a flight of stairs. Starlight went to a small room. Then someone came up quickly, blindfolded her and went away.

Chapter 5: Lost and Found

Starlight struggled until the ropes loosened. Starlight jumped up, unblindfolded herself, and saw Little Fox in a cage asleep. Starlight freed her brother, went out of the house and went back home.

Chapter 6: Catch the Evil Villain

Starlight's mom, Sweet Rose, was awake. She couldn't find Little Fox or Starlight. Then the door opened and Starlight came in. Her mother hugged them and Starlight told her the story, and they had a big feast. As for the shaman, she was never heard from again!

I was impressed by Sandra's first draft. She had a knack for writing fiction, especially mysteries. Her characters' actions made "people sense" most of the time, and she developed her plot with a sense of suspense. She worked on clarifying her story problem, changing the title of Chapter 1 from "Getting a Shiver" to "Where Is Little Fox?" after she created Little Fox for the ghost to kidnap.

But her piece also contained a number of anachronisms and unexpected responses. James thought it was important to discuss these details with her so that she could rethink and possibly revise her story, so he called her over for a conference at the beginning of the ninth day of writing.

MR. VENABLE: Sandra, I read your story last night, and I think it has a really nice plot. I'm wondering, do you see this story as taking place in Ohlone times?

SANDRA: Yeah, but you see, the machine, it was made out of what they had then. It wasn't made out of electricity like tape recorders and all that stuff.

MR. VENABLE: Well, that part is a bit confusing to me. When you say "machine" I think about a machine that works with levers and wheels. Is that what you mean?

SANDRA: Well . . . (*Long pause*)

MR. VENABLE: Do you think that the Ohlones had machines with levers and wheels?

SANDRA: Huh, no, I guess they wouldn't have.

MR. VENABLE: There's something else I'm wondering about. You mention houses in your piece. Could you tell me more about these Ohlone houses?

SANDRA: Well, it was, like, very small. It had upstairs and downstairs.

MR. VENABLE: The Ohlone house had an upstairs?

SANDRA: Well, this was only one house. It was small. It was like a sweathouse.

MR. VENABLE: You mention that the houses had windows and stairs. Do you think that the Ohlone houses had windows and stairs?

SANDRA: No, not really.

MR. VENABLE: I like the way you've written your piece, but there are things in it that don't seem Ohlone to me. Sometimes it seems like these are modern people—it seems that way when you talk about the houses and the machine. If you want to make this an authentic Ohlone story, you're going to have to make sure everything in it makes Ohlone sense. Or you can choose to make this a modern mystery story and take the Ohloneness out of it. You need to decide which kind of story you want to write. Think about it.

Sandra conferred with James again the following day. She told him she had decided to make an Ohlone story and revise the part about the house. Then she surprised us: later in the writing session, she abandoned her piece without revision and began a new Ohlone story. James thought she did this because he'd been too directive with her the day before.

But I wasn't sure. Sandra struck me as a flexible writer, and I couldn't imagine that revision posed a problem for her. So I asked her why she chose to start again, and she told me that she didn't think that her first story had "enough Ohloneness and it wasn't worth fixing it up." As she talked, I was impressed with her growing sense of the historical milieu. She went on to say that she had thought of a really good story that she liked even better. She wrote (also see her original handwritten draft, included as Writing Sample 3):

The Adventures of Sunset

Chapter 1: The Dead Ceremony
Sunset held her breath as the medicine woman tried to heal Sunset's cousin. "It's no use," the medicine woman said, "She's dead."

Sunset cried and Mountain Eagle said, "We'll have a ceremony tomorrow."

"Okay," Sunset said and went to bed.

It was a chilly night and Sunset still was awake. She felt cold and musty inside. She laid awake until the sun peaked through the hills. Sunset woke up and ate her breakfast slowly. After, she got dressed. She went out for the ceremony. They prayed and burned Sunset's cousin Moonlight's things. This was a tough moment for Sunset. She cried through the praying.

Sandra's new story was filled with Ohloneness. There were no machines or houses with stairs in this piece. This story was clearly set in the Ohlone milieu. James felt that she didn't need his help at this point, so he just let her write. She worked on her story for another week, conferring from time to time with Margaret and Joan. Later on, when I talked to her about her writing, she told me that she got very stuck about three days into her new piece.

> The part about the island of the dead was a place where I got real stuck. I had to represent Ohloneness in it, so that people would know it was an Ohlone story. I talked to Margaret, and she suggested that I keep talking about dead things. Then I was thinking, "Kids like this so maybe I should do this." I thought about it at home, and I thought about I should have Sunset wondering about dying. Then it went into my mind to do something else—I forget what it was. Then I thought about the book and I read a little more of *Little Bird* at school and thought about what the reader would be interested in. Then I wrote the next part.

I was impressed with Sandra's ability to think about how she wrote, despite her confusion about the origin of her historical ideas. She seemed to have a clear sense of audience as she crafted this piece, and she made conscious decisions about how to develop her Ohlone characters and elaborate on her story problem. When she was stuck, she considered two plot options, talked to a peer, read an Ohlone narrative, and decided to continue exploring Ohlone ideas about dying by having Sunset wonder about her own death. All of this made good writing sense, and it also made good historical sense.

James had a final conference with Sandra to refine her narrative, this time paying special attention to the "people sense" in her story. James felt that the events in the piece were logically connected but the characters needed development.

MR. VENABLE: You've got three characters in your piece: Sunset, Sweet Dove, and Sundance. I have trouble telling them apart sometimes. Is there something you can do about that?

SANDRA: Well, I don't know.

MR. VENABLE: In one place you introduce Sundance as Sunset's best friend. You might want to do more of that.

SANDRA: Sweet Dove is her friend, too. I could tell about that.

MR. VENABLE: Yes, that might work. And sometimes authors sprinkle descriptions of characters throughout the story. You might want to think about that. I think that would help me follow what happens in your story.

Sandra revised her piece once more (see the published version, included as Writing Sample 4 at the end of this section), trying to give her audience a finer sense of Sunset, Sundance, and Sweet Dove. She didn't describe the three girls, but she did try to explain their relationships by telling the reader that Sweet Dove was Sunset's "oldest friend."

James and I talked about the changes Sandra went through during the ten weeks of the workshop. Some of the artifacts and scenes from the narrative ended up in *The Adventures of Sunset,* but a lot of them did not. When I asked Sandra about this, she told me that she "learned things" about the Ohlones even though she didn't use most of the information in her piece. It's difficult to measure exactly what she had learned, but her talking, writing, and drawing contained a clearer sense of "Ohloneness" as the workshop progressed. I think that she abandoned her first story because it didn't make Ohlone sense to her anymore. If we had simply told Sandra about the Ohlones, I don't think this would have happened.

Sandra refined her sense of the Native American milieu and rethought her other historical ideas during the course of the workshop. At the end of the year, she still didn't have a very clear sense of what the rest of the world was like during Ohlone times, telling me that she "just didn't know." But our questions and Sandra's own reflections and explorations made her rethink some of her theories. And I wasn't surprised that she drew tule huts instead of tepees when she illustrated her book in April.

The msgtery of the house on Philpot Pathl

Chaper One. Getting a shiver

La la, de la, al, aLa said Starlight, hamming to herself. She
was picking acorn's with her mother. Suddley a white
thing flew towerds her' She scremed and it went
away. Her mother turned Why did you scremed she said
sounding agrey. Starlight looked at her sheepshliy
There was a ghost she replied. Oh said her mother

Writing Sample 1

The mystery of the house on Philpot Path!

1

Chaper One Where is Little fox?

La la de la la La said Starlight, humming to herself. She was picking acorn's with her mother. Suddley a white thing flew towerd's her! She scremed and it went away. Her mother turned Why did you scremed she said sounding (agrey) Starlight looked at her (sheepshly) There was a ghost she replied Oh said her mother and then went backpicking acorn's. When they were walking toweds home, Starlight thought, I will go in that house. Then they walked in the house. Some thing was wrong and it only took a second for Starlight to relized who it was! Little fox, her little brother was gone! Mom, Little Fox is gone. Starlight said. He'll be back tonight her mother

She laid awake for a long time.
Chaper two: The Sream!

The next morning was cold and gray Starlight woke up. Her mother was making breakfast. Did Little Fox come home, Starlight akded. No, her mother said crying. She wiped her tears and

Writing Sample 2

said to Starlight Go pick some berrie's please. So Starlig
went off. She (decied) to take a shortcut on
Philpot path. As she (apoched) it she herd a nosie. She came
towards it she herd a long harsh seasm that senda shiver
up Starlght's spine. Then she ran away.

Chaper three: Run Starlight Run

Starlight ran hope(less ly) with no idea where she was
going. When she stop she was lost! (Sunndley) she was took
at a face! Come here, the lady said redching
for her. Starlight duked and ran to the safety
of her. village.

Chaper four The Ghost Machine

When Starlight came home it was six.
Her mother was not angry (though). That night
Starlight got of her room and through the door and an door
Philpot Prat hand ran into the house.

As soon as she steped in she gasped. There was
machine's dummy and fake ghosts! Starlight grinned. So that's
where all the ghosts come from she thought. She saw
a flight of stair's. Starlight went to a small room Then somone
came up quickly, blind folded her and went away.

Writing Sample 2 (continued)

Starlight stuggled until the ropes loosened Starlight jumped up.
and blinded herslf and saw Little fox in a cage asleep Starlight freed
her brother went out the hose and went back home.
Chaper Six
Caeth the evil villon
Starlight's mom, Sweet Rose was awake. She couldn't
find little fox or Starlight. Then the door open and
Starlight came in. Her mother hugged them and Starlight
told the her the story and they had a big feast. As for
the showman she was never heard from agian!

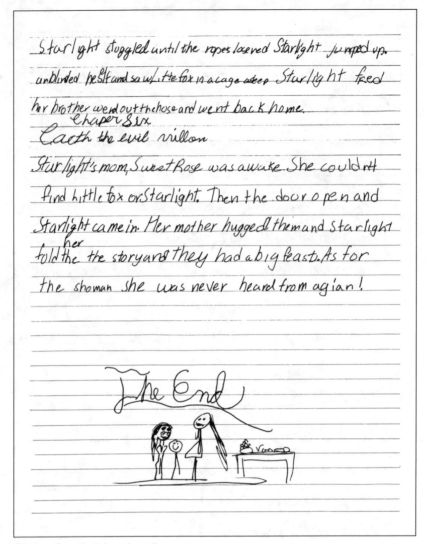

The End

Writing Sample 2 *(continued)*

The Adventures of Sun Set
Chapter One The dead ceromony.
Sunset held her breath as the medicene womin
try to heal Sunset's cosin. It's no use the medicene
woman said, she's dead. Sunset cried and
Mountain Eagle said we'lll have a ceromony
tomaroww. Okay Sunset said and went to bed
It was a chilly night and Sunseti still was awake.
She fell cold and musty inside.
She laid awake until the sun peaked though
the hills. Sunset woke up and ate her breakfast
slowly. After she got dressed she went outside
for the ceromong. They prayed and burned
Sunset's cosins, Moonlight things. Tho was a
tough moment for Sunset. She cried thourgh the
praying a

Writing Sample 3

THE ADVENTURES
OF
SUNSET

CHAPTER ONE:
THE DEAD CEREMONY AND
WONDERING

Sunset held her breathe as the medicine woman tried to heal Sunset's cousin. "It's no use," the medicine woman said, "she's dead."

Sunset cried and Mountain Eagle said, "We'll have a ceremony tomorrow."

"Okay," Sunset said and went to bed. It was a chilly night and Sunset still was awake. She felt cold and musty inside. She laid awake until the sun peaked through the hills.

Sunset woke up and ate her breakfast slowly. After she got dressed she went outside for the ceremony. They prayed and burned Sunset's cousin's (Moonlight) things.

This was a tough moment for Sunset. She cried through the praying and the burning. At the end she asked her mother, "Is Moonlight happy?"

"Yes, she is in the Island of the Dead," her mother replied.

"Huh?" Sunset said, "Where's that?"

"I'll tell you after supper," her mother said.

Supper was quieter than usual. They talked once in a while about the ceremony. Then it was just silence.

After supper Sunset and her mother sat on the floor. Her mother began, "The Island of the Dead is a place where dead spirits go. As you know," she said, "we burn the dead person's stuff so they never come back."

"When will I die?" Sunset said.

"I don't know. I just don't know," her mother said.

Sunset did not answer. She thought about why her cousin died. A mountain lion had attacked her. Mountain Eagle saw her and had brought her back. Sunset gulped. She never wanted to die that way. She just wanted to. . . to. . . die.

"Time for bed," her mother said interrupting her thoughts.

"Okay," Sunset said. She was fond of saying that. When she was in bed, she said her thoughts in her mind all over again.

CHAPTER 2:
LOST OVERNIGHT

"Hurry up, Sunset. Get dressed. It's late," her mother said.

Sunset got up and quickly got dressed. She wanted to pick acorns.

"Breakfast," her mother said.

Sundance, her best friend, called.

Sunset ate her breakfast and rushed out the door. She went through the village and into the woods. She was so excited – she walked right by the big Oak.

Sunset kept walking and stopped. She didn't know where she was. She tried to go back, but it was useless. She found a swimming hole. She swam a while, but then she got bored. She got into picking acorns, but then she got bored again. So she just sat down.

Sunset was not that scared. But when it was night, she got lonely and scared. Sunset said rather loudly, "Help!" It didn't work. She ate some berries. But then a thought came to her. "If she fell asleep, an animal could get her!"

Writing Sample 4

She started to run and stopped at the part where she got lost at. She was closer now to the village. She screamed, "Help!" It took awhile, but then Sunset heard footsteps. It was Sweet Dove her oldest friend.

"I heard your screams," she said quite calmly. "Let me take you home."

"Okay," said a voice.

They turned around and they were about to scream in Sundance's face. Sundance was calm and quiet. "Let's go home," she said. Then they all walked home together.

CHAPTER THREE:
SPYING

"Don't you think Leaping Rabbit is an evil shaman?" Sunset explained, "I mean no one goes in her house except her sister."

"What?" Sweet Dove said.

"Well, nobody sees her go in or out," Sunset replied.

"I think you're making something out of nothing." Sweet Dove said, "Your mind probably has a plan like spying, right?"

"Right!" Sunset replied.

"Well, then hurry up with your plan," Sweet Dove said. "She's so old, she'll probably die."

"What," Sunset burst out. "You aren't going to help me spy?"

"That's right," Sweet Dove said.

"Oh, please," Sunset pouted.

Sweet Dove hated her friend pouting. "I'll do it," she said.

"Okay!" Sunset said, "Here's the plan. We'll go sneak out at night, go to her house, and peer inside and see if she's doing anything weird!"

"Good plan! Let's go home." Sweet Dove said.

"Wear dark clothes like black bear fur," Sunset said and they left.

The night was crisp and cold as Sunset sneaked out of the house and went to Sweet Dove's house.

"Are you ready," she said.

"Ready!" Sweet Dove said and off they went.

"You're going so slow," Sunset said.

"I know," Sweet Dove said.

As they approached the house and just as they were going to peek inside, the fur door flew open and out came Leaping Rabbit's sister!

"Well, look at what we have here." she said. "Come inside."

They came inside because they were really cold. There was Leaping Rabbit asleep.

"Don't get close to her." Her sister said, "She's sick"

"Oh, is that why she never comes in and out?" Sweet Dove asked sweetly.

"Yes," her sister said.

"See!" Sweet Dove said turning around, sticking her tongue at Sunset.

"Would you two like some fish?" Leaping Rabbit's sister said.

"Sure," they replied and sat down and ate salmon.

Then it got late and Sunset and Sweet Dove said goodbye and went home. In her sleep Sunset said to herself, "Leaping Rabbit is not bad!"

CHAPTER FOUR:
SICK FROM THE RAIN

"Hurry up, Sweet Dove!" Sunset said. They were going exploring, but lately Sunset was talking about how slow Sweet Dove was or what a slow-poke Sweet Dove was or something like that.

Suddenly they hear a clang of thunder as it started to rain.

Writing Sample 4 (continued)

"Don't worry, Sweet Dove. Hurry though," Sunset said with a smile. They raced back to the village and got inside. Sunset started coughing. She coughed all week and she got a terrible cold. Her parents had nothing to trade with Leaping Rabbit, the shaman, who had gotten well.

So Leaping Rabbit came over. After examining her, she looked up and said, "I think the rain has done this."

She got plants and tried to heal her. It took ten moons to heal her. Then Leaping Rabbit looked up and said, "She's cured!"

Sunset looked around and got up and went over to Sweet Dove's house and said, "The rain's stopped. Let's go exploring."

CHAPTER FIVE:
LAST DAY

One day Sunset said in a cheerful voice, "I think I'll go pick some acorns today."

Her friends came along. After what seemed like a long time, Sweet Dove and Sundance came back and said, "Sunset got lost! We can't find her!"

Two days passed and she didn't come back. Her mother started to worry and went to bed crying every night.

Leaping Rabbit joined the search. Now when her mother was outside, she began to cry right in front of people! Lots of people were searching.

Then one day a young woman found her by some rocks, deep in the forest. Claw marks had pierced her heart. They had a ceremony. Her mother cried and said, "I don't think she wanted to die that way, like her cousin, but she did."

The End

Writing Sample 4 (continued)

Elizabeth

• • • • • • • • • •

I used to see Elizabeth in the hallways. She struck me as flamboyant, sometimes wearing old black hats and men's secondhand vests to school. She always seemed to be chattering with a group of girls. She exuded energy, even mischievousness. I could tell the other kids liked her—she had funny things to say and enjoyed saying them. Sometimes this got her into trouble, but teachers liked her. I liked her. She was bright, creative, and had a wonderful sense of humor.

I didn't focus my attention on Elizabeth until well into the turn-of-the century workshop when she started having difficulties with her piece and kept asking for conferences. The more I talked with her, the more I wondered about her historical understanding and her writing. I found myself talking to her daily, listening and watching to see how she solved her writing problems and what she thought about late-nineteenth-century urban life.

Elizabeth chose a biography of Alexander Graham Bell to read during the first week of history workshop. She told me she'd chosen it "because I'd heard a lot about Alexander Graham Bell, and I wanted to know more about telephones. They interest me. Inventions interest me." She also read David Macaulay's *Castle,* because "I'd already read part of it in GATE [the Gifted and Talented Education program], but we didn't have a chance to go over all of it." Elizabeth seemed interested in these books, but I sensed that she might have selected nonhistorical works if I had given her the choice. She told me later that realistic contemporary fiction was her "very favorite."

Elizabeth's understanding of life in 1900 didn't surprise me. At the very beginning of the workshop, she seemed to have a clear sense of the milieu. She wrote in her response log: "All the women wore large, puffy, itchy, flowery dresses with hard to manage hoops. There were little or no cures for diseases, no automobiles. Horse-drawn carriages." What else did she know? I wasn't sure at this point, but she asked in her log whether "1900" meant "cowboy time or Victorian?" Elizabeth's question was sophisticated. Cowboys and Victorian city dwellers lived simultaneously in different places in the United States. Her question told me that she visualized a complex 1900 milieu. I probed for more information a few days later while Elizabeth drew scenes from the turn of the century. She told me that her 1900 house "is not to scale and not geometric. I know that my house looks completely odd. This is supposed to be a drawing of a Queen Anne with a starburst window above the door."

Elizabeth's milieu drawing was remarkable. I knew that she studied Victorian architecture in a "gifted and talented" pullout class, but I was impressed that she remembered to include a house in the Queen Anne style in her 1900 street scene. The rest of her drawing showed a similar attention to historical detail, including dirt roads and a general store, ladies with bustles, carriages, and school desks with inkwells. "What did the rest of the world look like when Alameda's streets were lined with Victorian houses?" I asked her, because I wondered how her understanding differed from Sandra's and that of the other fifth graders in Janet's room.

> This drawing was supposed to be an Alameda or Oakland-type place. Like, maybe the rest of the United States might not have looked like that. San Francisco was a major city. Berkeley and Oakland were considered suburbs of it. New England, I read a book about it, might have had houses with thatched roofs there because the thatched roofs worked so well. They might have also had brick houses because there were no earthquakes there. When I picture Mexico, I think that people might have lived in villages. There was a big city but people preferred to live in small villages within about a five-mile radius of it, scattered. I think Paris would have been much more impressive than here. They had large stone monuments like the Arc de Triomphe. . . . I think they would have cars, old cars. They also had horses and carriages and they probably had a metro with small noisy engines and some of them might have been pulled by horses.

Elizabeth saw the turn-of-the-century world as diverse and complex. In some places she envisioned big cities with early metro systems; in others she saw an urban area surrounded by rural countryside and small villages. Sandra visualized complexity as well, but Elizabeth's sense of the milieu was more detailed, and she was able to articulate how she knew all this. She said that "it was easy to get a picture of Europe because I went there when I was in third grade, when I was eight. I knew that Napoleon was there for quite a while, and he built lots of buildings." She told me that she read about New England in books and remembered old Mexico from magazine photographs.

Elizabeth was playful and talked almost constantly when she explored the artifacts at the centers. Her history talk was an animated mix of analysis and pretending. I saw her role-play with Dorothy, pretending she was ironing an imaginary blouse that Dorothy then "slipped" over her T-shirt. The next day she and Dorothy imagined that they were preparing waffles at the center containing kitchen items. Elizabeth explained in her log that she "pretended that my hand was a waffle." She commented that she wanted to go to the clothing center next and then hear the oral history at the listening center. Over the next few days she visited both of these areas, remarking that the clothing center "was cool, but it would have been better if all the boys in my group [hadn't] hogged all the clothes." Elizabeth listened intently to the oral history tape and told me later that she thought it was painful for the old woman I interviewed to talk about her childhood.

The following week Elizabeth read about "cars and old bikes that were really funny." She told Janet that we ought to call old-fashioned cars "dust cars, because you get dusty when you ride in it." She commented that she'd seen old cars in France. The next day, Elizabeth went to the clothing table and read about hats and fashions, remarking that "some were frumpy, yet others were very chic." She seemed particularly interested in clothing and read books about fashion for two days. She gathered information and then, as she frequently did, generalized in her log about what she'd learned:

"Basically, I think they thought that the more fluff, puff, ribbons and lace, the better the look."

I was curious to see what would happen on our first day of writing. Elizabeth had a sophisticated sense of history, she was obviously very bright and inquisitive, but she had trouble writing. Janet told me that Elizabeth often experienced sustained writer's block, and some of her teachers thought that the block was the result of a learning disability. I noticed that her response log entries were short, especially when I compared them with Sandra's flowing responses and with the responses of other, less sophisticated fifth graders in Janet's room. But I knew that writing entries in a response log was different from storywriting; as was true of a number of other students, much of Elizabeth's thinking wasn't showing up in her log. The brevity of her entries didn't tell me much about her other writing, but I still wondered whether she would be able to break some of her old writing patterns.

When the day came to write, Elizabeth spent a long time whispering to Dorothy and Sophia about her ideas. For forty minutes she talked to them and struggled with a number of leads, all for stories with different problems. She ended up with three beginnings, finally settling on an idea during the last five minutes of the session. Her first attempt: "It was terrible. Jane had fallen sick. Mother called all the housewives nearby. They all rushed right over." Her second attempt: " 'Okay, whose got my jacks?' thought Betty as she started for the door." Her third attempt (shown in Writing Sample 5 at the end of this section): " 'My brothers are so mean!' thought Betty as she started for the door. 'All I wanted was to borrow pants, so I could take turns with Mary-Beth riding her brother's bike.' "

I conferred with a number of other students before I talked to Elizabeth. No one else in the class was writing about girls' wearing pants in 1900, although eleven students had started stories involving games and sick children. We had four or five minutes before the bell rang, and I wanted to ask Elizabeth about her story idea, but as we talked, I discovered that she was stuck and decided to help her talk about the "people sense" in her piece.

MS. JORGENSEN: How's it going?

ELIZABETH: Actually, this started out different. I put the wrong title on it. That's (*Pointing to the lead of her third attempt*) what it's going to be about.

MS. JORGENSEN: What's your piece about?

ELIZABETH: It's about a girl who tries to steal her brother's knickers so she can ride a bike.

MS. JORGENSEN: This wasn't your first idea?

ELIZABETH: Well, I started with this story about the girl getting sick, and then I did the jack story. But I didn't do a jack story because I couldn't get it. I couldn't go on. But now I'm not sure where to go from here on this story.

MS. JORGENSEN: Why don't you read what you have so far. (*Elizabeth reads her lead*) I like your lead. It makes me want to hear more. Do you have any idea about why you're stuck here?

ELIZABETH: I can't think of what Betty does next.

MS. JORGENSEN: It might help to talk about Betty. What kind of person is she?

ELIZABETH: She's kind of like, "I don't care what others think of me. I want to do this, so I'm going to do it."

MS. JORGENSEN: Does she live in a family?

ELIZABETH: She has two older brothers, a younger sister, a mother, a father, and a grandma who lives upstairs.

MS. JORGENSEN: Are any of these people going to be important in the story?

ELIZABETH: I'm not sure. I just made up the family as I went along.

MS. JORGENSEN: Let's think about them for a minute. How do you think these people would react if Betty took the knickers?

ELIZABETH: Her brother just laughs at her when she wants to borrow a pair of pants. Her mother doesn't know yet, and she hasn't told her because she knows that her mother will disapprove. And her father works, so she can always be home before he is. But she knows that he can't find out because he would be really mad.

MS. JORGENSEN: How about the grandma?

ELIZABETH: The grandma is sick, and she lives upstairs, far away. I don't think she will be important.

MS. JORGENSEN: You said she started for the door. Where is she?

ELIZABETH: She started for the door out of the bedroom. She lives on the floor on which there's the nursery. Her brothers are twins. They are one year older and live in a room next to hers. Also on that floor there are two other bedrooms and a small bathroom.

MS. JORGENSEN: What's going to happen next? She walks out the door and . . .

ELIZABETH: Well, it's the door to her bedroom, and I think that what she's probably going to do is to have what she considers to be a wicked idea, which is to go into her brother's room and borrow his pair of pants without his permission.

MS. JORGENSEN: So you have to get her to his room. Any ideas on how to do that?

ELIZABETH: Not yet. I'm stuck.

MS. JORGENSEN: Think about it.

I hoped our conversation would help Elizabeth get over this first writing block, but the going was slow. It took four days for her to write the next three sentences. Similar fluency problems plagued Elizabeth throughout the rest of the workshop. She wrote in spurts, often getting stuck for a week at a time in between. And I couldn't help but notice how different Elizabeth's and Sandra's writing processes were. Sandra was two years younger and equally bright, but she approached writing with great confidence, producing a large amount of thoughtful text in a short amount of time. I wondered how much of Elizabeth's problem was related to her "learning disability" and how much of it was related to the writing experiences she'd had since first grade. I wondered if she was ever given the opportunity to work through these blocks, to find her own ways of solving her writing problems.

On the seventh day of writing, Elizabeth asked for a conference. I had been too busy with other students to notice whether she had started writing again, so I was eager to talk with her. She told me that she wasn't quite sure what to write next.

ELIZABETH: The only thing is that I don't know where to take it after I say that they don't know where the brother keeps his pants and how they are going to find out without [her brothers'] knowing. Betty wants to get them but basically needs help getting them because she doesn't know where they are, and she's going to try to come in the morning while they're getting dressed to see which drawer they're in.

MS. JORGENSEN: So your next scene might be Betty trying to find out where they are?

ELIZABETH: Yes, or she might try to go in when they aren't there and open their drawers.

MS. JORGENSEN: Sounds like you need to think it out.

ELIZABETH: I guess you have to go paragraph by paragraph.

I left her for a while, hoping our talk would help her write. I conferred with other students and then returned to see how she was doing. She was still stuck. She told me that "Mary has a plan but I don't know what it is yet." I suggested that she talk to another student. She seemed reluctant but said she would try it. Two days later she told me that she still couldn't figure out what to write next but turned down my suggestion that she ask for help during our whole-group share. She was stuck, really stuck.

I puzzled over what to do next. Would talking into a tape recorder help? I caught her in the hallway a few days later and asked her if she wanted to try it. She agreed, and I gave her a tape to take home for the weekend. I didn't talk to Elizabeth for a couple of days, but the next time I read her piece, I saw that she had solved the problem. This is what she wrote:

"Still," replied Betty, "I don't know how to get my brother's knickers. And if he caught me . . ."

"Okay, I've got a plan. Let's go."

"Go where?" asked Betty.

"Your house," replied Mary, shrugging.

"Why? What are we going to do? We'll be caught, I know it!" whimpered Betty.

"No we won't. I've got it all planned," replied Mary.

"Stop," said Betty, "I'll not move another inch until you tell me what we're doing."

"Okay, my plan is this. We sneak into Paul's room, search it, and are out before he gets home," summed up Mary.

"Alright," sighed Betty, "let's go." She paused. "But if we're caught . . . I'll never speak to you again!"

"Trust me," said Mary. "We won't be caught!"

Elizabeth had solved her problem by having Mary, Betty's friend, propose that the girls sneak into the brother's room, search it, and take the knickers. Not the cleverest solution, but a solution nevertheless, and I wanted to find out whether talking into the recorder had helped. The next time I was in the room, I asked Elizabeth if we could have a conference.

MS. JORGENSEN: I see you solved the problem with finding the brother's knickers and you're writing again.

ELIZABETH: Have you heard my new intro? " 'My brother is so mean!' thought Betty as she started for the door. 'Sure, I know girls aren't supposed to wear knickers, but Paul had no reason to hide them. Now Mary and I can't have any fun.' "

MS. JORGENSEN: I really like your new lead. It sets up the historical problem very clearly. I'm also wondering if the tape recorder helped you continue your writing.

ELIZABETH: I found that the tape really didn't help me. It helped to get the idea, but listening to the tape didn't help, in fact listening to the tape made me really not like the way my story sounded. I guess I was reading it in a very flat and expressionless tone, and I was overacting it sometimes.

MS. JORGENSEN: What did you say on the tape?

ELIZABETH: I tried talking about what I would do next. Then I tried just putting my story aside and just using the basic plot line. I just recorded sentences that came to my mind.

MS. JORGENSEN: Did that help?

ELIZABETH: A little, but it turned out sounding a bit odd. I thought the tape recorder would help, but it didn't. Then I took a couple of days during writing where I just listened to other people's pieces and I think reading other people's pieces and seeing that other people were stuck, too, helped me. I read Keith's piece and I read Sophia's piece. She was really stuck when I read it on where to go next—she'd just gotten the setting, of how it was a beautiful, cold morning and the sun was rising—and she didn't know where to go from there. I asked her, "What's the best way that you can think of to switch into the earthquake?" And we sort of brainstormed it together, and for some reason that really helped me, I think, even though it wasn't nearly related to my piece.

Ms. JORGENSEN: Can you think of a reason why it helped to find out that other writers were stuck, too?

ELIZABETH: Knowing that they were stuck on their piece like I was and finding out that others were having trouble, they had a good beginning but didn't know where to go from there. I think that knowing that others had a problem and brainstorming with them really helped me.

I saw this as a breakthrough for Elizabeth. She had worked through a writing block. My suggestions probably helped, but I think the most important thing I did was to leave her alone so that she could sort it out for herself. On her own, Elizabeth discovered that getting stuck was a natural part of writing. Her conferences with Keith and Sophia helped her feel a part of a community of writers. Later on, she got stuck on her title and her ending, but she worked through these experiences with greater confidence and ease.

I knew when I read Elizabeth's piece that I needed to talk to her about whether her story made historical sense. I hadn't raised the issue before because I felt it was important for her to get over her writing block first. But her confidence had grown, and I decided I would address the historical content of her story in our next conference. That opportunity came a few days later.

Ms. JORGENSEN: Elizabeth, how's it going?

ELIZABETH: Pretty good. I'm working on, here, where Betty and Mary are sneaking into the house.

Ms. JORGENSEN: We haven't talked about this too much yet, but I was wondering what in your piece tells us that Betty and Mary live around the turn of the century?

ELIZABETH: The girls wanted to wear knickers and they weren't supposed to. The boys wear knickers and Mary's brother works in a general store. And I'm just about ready to write more about the Victorian house, the service porch.

Ms. JORGENSEN: Yes, that all makes good turn-of-the-century sense to me. There's one part that I'm wondering about. Do you think that a boy would have thrown away a pair of knickers if he got one stain on them at the turn of the century?

ELIZABETH: Well (*Long pause*), but he can't wear them, that's the thing.

Ms. JORGENSEN: What did you say his mom told him to do with them?

ELIZABETH: What if I just leave that part out?

Ms. JORGENSEN: Does the part about throwing them out make historical sense?

ELIZABETH: I really don't know.

Ms. JORGENSEN: Well, it doesn't make sense to me, because my guess is that most kids wore their clothes out. That's one of the reasons I had so much trouble finding children's clothing for the workshop.

ELIZABETH: (*Crosses out a phrase*) How about "I know he won't wear his dark green knickers because they've got a stain and he isn't allowed to wear them to work"?

MS. JORGENSEN: That makes more historical sense to me. So far your piece makes a lot of historical sense. Let's talk more tomorrow.

Elizabeth's story did make a great deal of historical sense. She consciously added details to help the reader visualize the early 1900s. By the end of her piece, she'd dressed Betty in the petticoat she researched at the clothing center and described her Victorian bedroom, complete with a bay window and window seat. Historical writing seemed to come easily to her, and I was surprised when she told me she thought it was hard to recreate the past. She said she used lots of dialogue in this story, more dialogue than she used when she wrote stories set in modern times:

> I guess I find it hard to convey the kids' thoughts without using dialogue. It's like in my historical writing, I use a bunch of dialogue, whereas in my other fictional writing I don't use that much. I think I do that because it was hard for me to see what's going on in my historical fiction. It's easy for me to see "today." It's like, how do we really know what happened back then? How do we really know how the artifacts were used?

Elizabeth was amazingly sophisticated. I didn't expect a fifth grader to think so profoundly about the nature of historical writing. She wanted her characters to make historical sense, but she had trouble seeing the world through their eyes. "How do we really know what happened back then?" What a good question.

The end of the fifth-grade workshop felt rushed. Janet was very flexible, but the writing had taken longer than I had anticipated. I wanted another week, but I had set a deadline for publication so that we could hold our history author celebrations before things got too hectic at the end of the school year. Elizabeth felt rushed, too. She wasn't a fluent or prolific writer, and she needed time to work through her writing blocks. When we got down to the wire, she felt pressured to end her story without resolving the conflict. We talked about her ending after her piece was edited and typed (her final handwritten draft is included here as Writing Sample 6):

> You know where, at the end of the story, where [Mary] tells her the plan to get into Paul's room? Well, after that, I got most of it finished and then I said to myself: "Elizabeth, you're almost finished. You just have to wrap it up. If you wrap it up, you can get it typed, and it will look nicer in a book." I really wanted to finish it, and I think that's really one of the reasons I took the cop-out. I'm sure I could have solved Betty's problem, but I couldn't do it without making it a really, really, really long piece, which I didn't have time to do.

Elizabeth thought her ending was a cop-out because her initial premise was still unresolved. But she was more distressed about this than I was, because I felt she had learned a great deal about herself during the workshop. She learned that getting stuck was a part of writing. She also learned about fiction. Like Sandra, Elizabeth had a knack for it. My job was to provide opportunities for her to talk about her writing. I knew if she talked about it, she'd discover that her writing was very effective. Elizabeth needed to know that she was a good writer in order to become a fluent writer. In one conference, she initiated a discussion about a nicely crafted section of her story:

ELIZABETH: Do you know what my favorite passage is? "All of a sudden, the step that Betty was standing on issued a creak. With a flash of inspiration Betty yanked Mary by the hand, and at the same time she pressed a finger to her lips."

MS. JORGENSEN: Why do you like that part?

ELIZABETH: So much is happening, but you get a very vivid picture of exactly what is happening. Because the step just gave a creak and if they are not careful, they're going to get caught. They're really scared.

MS. JORGENSEN: How do we know they're scared?

ELIZABETH: Because before that Betty said, "If we're caught, I'll never speak to you again." Then she *yanks* Mary's wrist, otherwise she could have just taken her by the hand and just led her, but here she grabbed Mary by the wrist. "Yanked" is a quicker movement.

MS. JORGENSEN: How does that quick movement make the reader feel?

ELIZABETH: I think it makes me feel that, like, everything has to be done quickly, and they have to get out of there. The reason she pressed her finger to her lips is that in case Mary didn't understand she might say, "Why are you grabbing my wrist. What's the matter?" and she might start talking rather loud, and the mother might hear her, and they might get caught.

MS. JORGENSEN: What's the pace of the action in this scene?

ELIZABETH: Fast.

MS. JORGENSEN: I think so, too. You create a lot of tension and suspense in this part of your story. The action is very fast and it all kind of happens simultaneously—yanking her hand almost at the same time she puts her finger to her lips. The way you wrote this part helps me know how tense this is for Betty and Mary.

Elizabeth knew this part of her story was good, and I wanted her to discover why she liked it so much. She had selected her words carefully, juxtaposing two actions and building tension in her piece. Both of us identified with her characters and empathized with their feelings as they moved up the stairs. This was fine writing, and it provided me with an opportunity to reinforce Elizabeth's confidence in her own natural abilities.

Elizabeth learned something else during the workshop. She rethought her view of the past after weeks of exploring firsthand sources, writing, talking, and drawing. By the end of the workshop, she had refined her turn-of-the-century milieu, deciding that cowboys and Victorians probably lived at the same time. In May I asked her how she would change her drawing if she were to do it again. She told me the street scene she'd pictured wasn't exactly the same as the streets she saw in the 1900 photographs at the centers:

> I'd put in [sic] a bakery in it because there were bakeries back then. I'd change the general store because it looked more like a mining town. I would stay with what the people wore. I might give the woman a hat and a shawl. I'd give the little boy a cap. I wouldn't draw a really young child, because it would be kind of confusing, a little bald kid wearing a dress.

The workshop helped Elizabeth see "1900" differently. Writing her story about clothing taboos also helped her rethink how she defined a historical event. This issue came up in a writing conference during which we looked back at her piece and talked about how it fit into the class's reconstruction of 1900. As we talked, Elizabeth revised her ideas about what events are significant enough to be called "history." She began with the theory that only "important events that change something" are history. Those events, she reasoned, were defined by textbooks. This made sense to me. In fourth and fifth grades, Elizabeth learned textbook history. She learned that California and the United States were molded by political and economic events. Although our workshop covered economic and political issues, it focused on social history, the history of everyday life.

MS. JORGENSEN: When we put all of our writing together, we ended up with a history of 1900. What do you think history is?

ELIZABETH: History is important events that change something. The invention of the telephone, an important event. People could get messages faster and they could say them to the person instead of just having a piece of paper.

MS. JORGENSEN: Your story is about children's clothes. Is that a part of history?

ELIZABETH: No, because girls wear pants now. When I think of history, it has to be in a textbook. The kind of history has to be important. History is not so much "It happened to me today" so that's history. That's not my idea of history. My idea is like someone—Columbus—discovers America. That's history.

MS. JORGENSEN: So what people wore is not a part of history?

ELIZABETH: Well, I think it could be history, but you're not going to open a history text and read about it. Unless it was a history book in minute detail. Some things are history because they happen. They tell us how it happens. These are my two definitions of history.

I sensed that Elizabeth was uneasy about her new theory. She needed one definition of history, a definition that included social, economic, and political events. I trusted that this would come later. She was reflective, and I knew she would eventually see that history was not defined by a text-book. She would discover that she had the power to define history for herself and that the process of rethinking the past would continue after the workshop ended.

Playing Jacks

"My brothers are so mean!"
thought Betty as she started for
the door. All I wanted was to
borrow pants so I could take
turns with Mary-Beth
riding her brothers' bike.

Writing Sample 5

"My brother 'is so mean!"
thought Betty, as she started for ~~a~~ _supose_
the door. "Suce I know girls aren't _to_
~~wear nickers, but Bun had no reason~~
~~to~~ hide them ~~Mary and~~ cau't
~~have his bro~~

"It's _Bun_ no fair!" Betty
wailed, "You get to wear

your brothers pants any
time you want?"
"No I don't. He

dosen't know I ~~borrow~~ _borrow_
them" ~~replied~~ Mary ~~~~
replied

The girls giggled ~~irreveriantly~~ for several
minutes, _until_ ~~until~~ Betty demanded to know,
"How do you get the nickers without your
brother finding out?"

"It's easy" replied Mary ~~Beth~~, "~~Betty~~ _Well_
keeps nickers at the end of his bed.
All I have to do is get into
his room and ~~snatch~~ _snatch,_ them. And
'cause ~~'caus~~ of his job at Mr. ~~~~ _Hatchers_
store. I know he won't ~~wear~~ _wear_ his
dark green nickers ~~because~~ _because_ they've
got a stain ~~and Mama said~~ he
~~should throw~~ ~~away but~~
~~he won't, but~~ she isn't _I Allowed_
to wear them, _either_ so they are ~~for~~ _basically_
the taking." ~~~~ finished Mary ~~~~

Writing Sample 6

ELIZABETH 113

When she was finished she was slightly out of breath yet both of them ~~laughed~~ LAUGHED. ~~any way~~. "Still," ~~replied~~ REPLIED Betty, ~~"I don't know~~ "I don't know how ~~they keep, get~~ ~~it did get~~ broth nickers. And

"Okay, I've got a plan. If ~~they~~ HE catch me ..." ~~lets go"~~ ~~"Tell her"~~

"Go where?" asked Betty.
"Your house." replied Mary ~~Mary~~ shrugging.
"Why? What are we going to do?"
"We'll be caught, I know it." whimpered Betty.
"No we won't. I've got it all planed." ~~replied~~ REPLIED Mary.
"Stop," said Betty, "I'll not move another inch ~~untell~~ UNTILL you tell me what we're doing."
"Okay my plan is this. We sneak into Paul's room, ~~search~~ SEARCH it, and are out before he gets home. ~~"~~ ~~Summed~~ SUMMED up Mary.
"Alright," sighed Betty, "Lets go." she paused. "But if were caught... I'll never speak to you again!"
"Trust me." said Mary. "We won't be ~~caught~~ CAUGHT !"

Fifteen minutes later, found them ~~keeping~~ CREAPING up the service stairway of Betty's house. All of a sudden the steps that Betty was standing on issued

Writing Sample 6 (continued)

a creak. With a flash of ineaperation Betty ~~grabbed~~ YANKED Marry by the hand. At the same time she pressed a finger to her lips. Marry understood, and ~~folowed~~ IMIDIATELY Betty into a bedroom. Betty whispered, "Quick under my bed!" Marry rolled under the bed lay still. Betty quickly smoothed her ~~dress~~, puffed her ~~petty~~ coats, & ~~strainned~~ STRAIGHTENED her hair. She ~~grabed~~ GRABBED her reader and ~~ploped~~ PLOPPED down in her bay window seat.

And not a moment ~~to~~ soon either. For just then Betty's mother poped her head in the door ~~& and~~ said, "Betty dear, ~~function~~ LUNCHEON is almost ready. Why don't you invite your little friend Marty?"

"Ok thank you Mommy! I'll go pay her a visit!"

Betty's mother left before she could hear a snicker come from under the cannopy bed.

The End

Writing Sample 6 (continued)

I didn't know Tanisha very well when she was in fourth grade, but she was hard to miss on the playground. She was very tall and one of the few African American students at Washington School. I always thought she carried herself well, especially when she was the occasional object of teasing. A group of fifth-grade girls in Janet's room sometimes kidded her about her height and called her "mommy," but she took it in stride.

Tanisha needed help with her reading in fifth grade. Since she was good with younger children, I put her in my peer tutoring program in October. She took her job seriously, helping a seven-year-old boy who was having reading problems. I got to know Tanisha during Friday tutoring meetings when we discussed teaching techniques and the progress of the second graders.

Tanisha was quiet in Janet's classroom. She sat in the very back, but I could sense her listening to me. She chose to read a biography of Martin Luther King when we began the workshop in March. She told me later that she thought she would use the book to help her write a story:

> I was going to write about Black people, and I wanted to know more about what really happened to Martin Luther King and how Black people, how they worked as slaves and stuff. . . . I stopped reading it because I wanted to write.

The independent reading library contained a number of books on African American history, but Tanisha chose to read other literature and never wrote a story clearly reflecting her heritage. For a while she redirected her energy to exploring the artifact centers. She spent a lot of her time quietly tinkering and poking, trying to figure out how the kitchen gadgets, tools, and odd objects functioned. She seemed fascinated with the centers, and I wasn't sure at that point how much she knew about the 1900 urban milieu. She said in her log that "they didn't have many things like we do." Then she pondered, "How come we have many [more] things than them and how come they didn't think of it first [since] they were here before?"

Tanisha's response told me that she knew that "things" were different in 1900, and she wondered why those "things" weren't invented before they were. How detailed was her idea of the 1900 milieu? I still didn't know. As I observed her at the centers, however, I was impressed by her curiosity. She was the first one in the class to open the 1910 folding camera. She worked on it for fifteen or twenty minutes and smiled broadly when she finally figured out how to move the small lever on the side and slide out the accordion front piece. But her written log response for that day didn't capture this small drama. She simply reported, "My [group] was [at center] four. It had a box thing, and I did not know what it was, but I opened it, and it was a camera."

Tanisha went back a number of times to the center with the cameras. At one point I saw her role-play briefly with Juanita, pretending she was taking

Juanita's picture. But most of her time was spent quietly reading and manipulating the cameras and tools. She remarked in her log that she read books about houses and cars "and found out that they had car seats and car horns, and one car horn was a golden dragon head. Then we looked at house books, and we saw pretty dining rooms and pretty tables." At another center she "only saw pictures, and we saw how the carriages looked."

I wondered what Tanisha would draw. She was obviously very curious about the artifacts, and I was impressed when she told me she wanted to read books so that she would have something to write about later in the workshop. But how did she visualize the 1900 milieu? It turned out that her turn-of-the-century family was a nuclear family with a mom, dad, and two kids. The mother's hair was piled high on her head, and she wore the same style dress as her daughter. I talked to Tanisha about her drawing.

MS. JORGENSEN: Tell me about your drawing of the 1900 family.

TANISHA: The lady has a pinklike dress with ruffles going down like that. The man—I used the vest in the back of the room and the hat. The little girl has a dress with blue and black checkers and comes up on her neck. The boy has a vest and big black boots.

MS. JORGENSEN: Where did you get these ideas?

TANISHA: I just thought of it.

MS. JORGENSEN: What about the school?

TANISHA: They had a small chalkboard. The kids are in straight lines and stuff and their desks don't open up and they had to put their books on the floor. I show how the teacher's desk was kind of like a table but it was a little small and she only had a little bit of papers on it and an apple.

MS. JORGENSEN: Anything else on the walls of your classroom?

TANISHA: Here's an alphabet and a world map.

MS. JORGENSEN: Why did you draw a small chalkboard?

TANISHA: I don't know. I just pictured a small chalkboard.

MS. JORGENSEN: Where did you get the idea for the school room?

TANISHA: I just thought like in 1900 they don't have desks like ours and stuff. They didn't have stuff that was made like ours.

MS. JORGENSEN: How did you decide what it would look like?

TANISHA: Like our classroom. In a book, I saw this school and the teacher wrote at the chalkboard and it was a little small.

MS. JORGENSEN: So the idea of the chalkboard came from a book?

TANISHA: And the desks in the book were running that way. I didn't know how to draw a bunch of desks.

MS. JORGENSEN: Did you get anything else from the book? (*Tanisha shakes her head*) What about your 1900 street scene? Tell me about that.

TANISHA: A lot of stores, a shoe repair store and stuff. There're big churches next to the houses.

MS. JORGENSEN: I notice that your houses look close together. Why did you draw them this way?

TANISHA: They're close together. They walk and they don't have to drive and everything is close by.

MS. JORGENSEN: Where did you get all of these ideas?

TANISHA: I read this book, and it had all kinds of stores in it, and it showed what stores looked like in 1800 and 1900. I read it a long, long time ago. There was this picture of a store with a man sitting in front of it making shoes. I can't remember the book.

Tanisha's drawing contained a fair amount of detail and few unexpected responses. What she knew about the milieu she learned from books and from the artifacts. She wasn't used to thinking about where she got her ideas, but when I probed she was able to tell me how she knew what she knew about the turn of the century. I wondered how she saw the rest of the world at this time, so I continued to ask questions.

MS. JORGENSEN: You drew a city in the United States in 1900. What do you think the rest of the world looked like?

TANISHA: (*Shakes her head*) I guess the same.

MS. JORGENSEN: Well, let's think. How about Paris or another city in Europe?

TANISHA: Probably looked different. Probably had newer buildings and stuff. Probably ate more things. Looked different. They probably remodeled a lot. If they have old stores they probably tore it down and put up another store or a house. Their houses are probably old, real old, where some of our houses were just being built. Right now we have more stuff, and it could hold up more.

MS. JORGENSEN: Do you think they had cars?

TANISHA: Not sure.

MS. JORGENSEN: What about Mexico?

TANISHA: (*Shakes her head*) I don't know.

MS. JORGENSEN: Can you picture any other part of the world at this time? (*Tanisha shakes her head*)

Tanisha understood that European cities were older than most American cities. "Their houses are probably old, real old," she theorized, "where some of our houses were just being built." But she seemed to know very little about the rest of the world. I was puzzled. She was curious, and on several occasions she quickly synthesized new information to refine her understanding. She used historical resources well, yet her view of the world and the United States in the early 1900s lacked detail. When I compared her responses with Elizabeth's, I couldn't help but wonder why Tanisha seemed to visualize so little.

Elizabeth traveled a lot with her parents. Tanisha's childhood was spent in the western part of the United States. Did this make a difference? What were her past experiences with historical materials? She tended to be a nonverbal, kinesthetic learner. Had she explored historical artifacts before?

She freely explored them during the workshop. Did this stimulate her to rethink her ideas? I decided to watch her closely and give her resources at every opportunity.

On the first day of writing, Tanisha couldn't think of a story idea. Tanisha, like Elizabeth, was not a fluent writer. She told me later that she finally got an idea after conferring with Janet. She said Janet had given a minilesson to the class the day before and asked them to visualize what it would be like to use the artifacts to do housework at the turn of the century. When she talked to Janet about her problem, Janet suggested that she think about the lesson and consider writing a story about an artifact. Tanisha told me that she looked around the room and decided to write about the flatiron and water pump. She was the only one in the class who wrote a story about a little girl doing household chores at the turn of the century. This was her piece at the end of the fourth day of writing (her handwritten draft is included at the end of this section as Writing Sample 7):

A Little Girl and Her Chores

There once was a little girl in the 1900s who had chores to do. She had to do the dishes by going out to get some water from a water pump. For the hot water, she had to boil some water and mix it with the cold water. Next she had to scrub the floors. She had to go back out to the water pump and get some more water and some soap and a scrub brush and go all around on the floors scrubbing. After that, she had to do ironing. She had to put the iron on a metal thing that is sitting over the fire and the iron is getting hot. The iron is hot and now she can begin to iron. When she is finished she starts to wash her clothes and she washes her clothes by using her hands. After she is finished washing her clothes, she starts to hang them. She hangs her clothes on a round thing and it has a long string wrapped around it to the other side. The other side has another round thing on it. She leaves the clothes out to dry and when they are dry she goes out to get the clothes and brings them into the house and folds them and puts them away neatly and then she can have the rest of the day to herself.

I read Tanisha's piece that evening. She didn't seem to have a problem getting her ideas down on paper, and it was clear that she had learned a great deal about what household chores were like in 1900. Her piece was full of historical information gleaned from books and artifacts, but it wasn't a story, even though she seemed to want to write one. Her piece was a list of activities, rather like a breakfast-to-bed story with no conflict or focal point. She created a character with no personality. The little girl in her story was a device to describe how the chores were done. I talked to Tanisha about this the next day.

Ms. JORGENSEN: How's it going?

TANISHA: Fine.

Ms. JORGENSEN: I read your piece last night. You've certainly written a lot, and you've put so much in your story that makes historical sense. Tell me some things you've written that help readers know that your story takes place in 1900.

TANISHA: . . . the chores. Like the pump with the water. Then she irons and puts the clothes out. She heats the water up.

Ms. JORGENSEN: Yes, those are all things someone would do in 1900 around the house. Who are the characters in your story?

TANISHA: A little girl.

Ms. JORGENSEN: Does she have a name?

TANISHA: No.

Ms. JORGENSEN: Are you going to create any other characters for your piece?

TANISHA: I don't know.

Ms. JORGENSEN: I was thinking that you might put a little excitement into your story by adding other characters and creating a problem for them to solve. The problem could be about doing the chores. Can you think of any other characters that you could add?

TANISHA: She could have a sister, a younger sister.

Ms. JORGENSEN: Okay. Anyone else?

TANISHA: A mom, they could have a mom.

Ms. JORGENSEN: That makes sense to me. Now what kind of problem could they have that involves the chores?

TANISHA: Maybe one of the sisters doesn't do her chores. She gets in trouble.

Ms. JORGENSEN: That would be one way to do it. Think about it—think about problems that they could have and then choose one to write into your story. Also, I think your characters would seem more real if they had names.

I wondered if Tanisha would follow my advice. She'd done a good job already, especially for someone who hated to write. But I wanted to see whether I could push her a bit further. I sensed that she was capable and needed a challenge. I wanted her to do more than just list chore descriptions. I wanted her to revise her piece, adding characters and developing a plot around a story problem. Could she do it?

A few days later, I noticed she was writing intently. Her first draft was at the top of her desk, and every few minutes she read a section from it and then wrote on another sheet of paper.

Ms. JORGENSEN: Looks like you're revising your story.

TANISHA: Next, I'm going to tell about how she teaches her sister how to iron.

Ms. JORGENSEN: Oh, so you put other characters in your story? What are their names?

TANISHA: The big sister's Sara. The little one's Suzanne.

Ms. JORGENSEN: Is there a mom?

TANISHA: The mom's going away so they have to do all the chores.

Ms. JORGENSEN: Is that the story problem?

TANISHA: (*Smiling*) Yes, I'm taking the first one and adding it to the second story.

MS. JORGENSEN: Is this story more fun to write?

TANISHA: (*Smiling again*) Yes. I like it better.

Tanisha was excited about her new story. She wrote constantly, without conferring or talking to other students. She had significantly revised her first draft by the end of the writing period (her handwritten revision is included as Writing Sample 8).

The Girls and Their Chores

Once there was a mother, and she had two little girls. The oldest was Sara. She was eleven years old, and Suzanne she was eight years old. Their mother had to go away to get some more food, and it was very far away. She said she might take two days to get there and back. She wanted Sara to teach Suzanne how to do chores, so that both of them can take care of the house.

Suzanne wanted to do chores since she was seven years old, but all her mother kept saying was that when she gets older she can do chores like Sara. When Sara told Suzanne that she had to teach her how to do chores, she was so happy that she could not wait to begin. Sara said, "When mother leaves, you can start."

The next day, the mother was getting ready to leave. She gave Sara and Suzanne a kiss, and as she walked out the door, they stood there until they did not see her. So Sara closed the door, and her and Suzanne got to work. Sara said, "We will start with the dishes."

Sara told Suzanne to follow her. "To get the cold and hot water to make warm water, you have to go to the water pump and that will be for the cold water and come back and get another bucket of water, and that will be for the hot water. But you have to boil some water and mix it together. Then after that, we can start to scrub the floors and to do that you have to come back out to get some more water and get the scrub brush from out of the kitchen and some soap and just scrub all around the floors.

Suzanne seemed to enjoy this, and she just could not wait to start. She asked Sara, "When can I start?"

"When I finish teaching you how to do it," said Sara. "Next, after you do the floors, you and I can do some ironing. This is how we are going to do it . . ."

Tanisha had transformed her piece. Her new characters had names and personalities, and they had a real story problem to solve. Tanisha turned her voiceless ironing and washing descriptions into dialogue. I knew that some of the language was awkward and her setting was unclear, but we could work on that later.

On the eighth day, Tanisha told me that she was "getting to the end" of her story. Two days later, I talked to her briefly, and again she told me that she had added "some stuff" but that she was almost finished. A day later she was still writing, commenting in her log: "I need to work on my ending, so it can be more interesting." She'd never written so much. Was she having a hard time ending it? When I asked her, she said, "I want to keep going on. I just like the way it feels."

Page by page, day by day, Tanisha discovered that she was a writer. She enjoyed the powerful feeling created by her newfound fluency, and she wasn't worried about ending her piece. I didn't rush her, but I was faced with a dilemma. The more she wrote, the more historical problems appeared in her story. I encouraged her to continue to explore history resources during the course of her writing, and she used them well, but a variety of subtle problems began to emerge. At one point in her story, for instance, the mother "turns off the light." In another section the sisters throw a boy-girl party that sounds suspiciously contemporary. By the twelfth day, I decided to focus on one major issue, hoping to get her to rethink some of her details without discouraging her obvious progress. I conferred with her toward the end of the writing period.

Ms. Jorgensen: How's it going?

Tanisha: Page sixteen!

Ms. Jorgensen: Great! What are you writing about now?

Tanisha: Sara's working in the store earning lots of money. Timothy's doing the chores.

Ms. Jorgensen: Oh, your story is getting very involved. You've done a really great job, and I thought we could talk a little about an important historical idea in your story. Tell me about the part in your piece where the family builds a store.

Tanisha: They build a store, and more people start moving out there—it's like in the woods, and they chop trees down and it opens up a big old space and people start to move in and build more houses, and they build a school for the kids and stuff and more people started moving in and they get customers because the clothes they sell are clothes that get too small for them and her mother makes clothes and they sell them, too.

Ms. Jorgensen: Sounds like people start moving there because the family built a store. How do the other people find out about the store?

Tanisha: (*Shrugging her shoulders*) I just thought because the mother . . . I don't know.

Ms. Jorgensen: It's an important question, and I think you need to think about it. There are reasons why towns and cities grow. I can understand people coming to live near the family and clearing the woods, but it doesn't make sense to me that they would come just because they heard there was a store there. Can you think of any other reason why people would come to this area in the woods?

Tanisha: Well, I think people started to move their houses. They were hungry so they started to move out there. And that's when they started to make the store because the family was running out of money.

Ms. Jorgensen: Okay. Sounds like the store came after a lot of people started moving there. That makes more sense to me. And your idea that other people moved there because they were hungry kind of reminds me of people moving west, looking for better farmland and a better life. Is this what you mean?

TANISHA: The people before they moved were getting put out of their houses so they left.

MS. JORGENSEN: And why did they pick this place in the woods to go to?

TANISHA: It's a nice space, maybe?

MS. JORGENSEN: You're on the right track. Think about it some more and I'll try to talk to you again today.

This was a complex historical issue. I hoped Tanisha would think about it and revise her piece. In the days that followed, she produced another twenty-four double-spaced pages. During this period, she finally decided to change the story and locate the family's house near a road, the road the mother took when she went to town to get food at the beginning of the story. This explained the growth of the town, she told me, because "the people knew about them because they went on the road."

She had another problem to solve. Her piece was long, and I talked to her about dividing her story into a sensible number of chapters. I gave her guidelines, suggesting that she look for story parts that had a clear beginning and ending. It took her two or three days to find seven chapters. She later told me that this was the most difficult part of the writing because she "got mixed up of where to stop for the next chapter." She solved the problem by "just reading up to it until it sounded right to start the next chapter."

Finding the chapters was difficult for her, but she did it. During the course of the workshop, Tanisha worked her way through other difficult problems. She learned that she could write fluently. I talked to her about this in June. Tanisha said that it was easy for her to write because her piece was historical. I also wondered if her story was partly autobiographical. After all, writers draw on their experiences to create fiction, and I saw autobiographical elements in much of the writing emerging from the two classrooms. When I had thought she was ready to end her piece, she had introduced Timothy into the plot, on the eighth day of writing. Now I understood why she kept writing. Timothy was really Tanisha's younger sister. He brought new momentum to her piece, helping her to create the last thirty pages of her story.

MS. JORGENSEN: How did you feel when you realized that you could write such a long piece?

TANISHA: I felt happy. I wanted to keep going on.

MS. JORGENSEN: I know that this is the longest piece you've written. Why do think that happened?

TANISHA: Because it was like a story about history. There's a lot of things about history you could put into a story. The other stories, if they were about history, they probably would have been as much. And when it's just a story, you can't get much things, details and stuff. . . .

MS. JORGENSEN: Were any of the characters in your story special to you?

TANISHA: Timothy, because I was like that when I was eight or nine. My sister had to show me how to do it.

MS. JORGENSEN: Is there anything else in your story that was like your life?

TANISHA: Well, when we turned about nine or ten, my mom teached us how to do chores. Now she rests and stuff while her kids do chores. Now my sister is starting to do chores. She needs to. She goes around saying, "Ha, ha, you have to clean up, and I get to go outside." Timothy, he reminds me of my sister. I told my mother that in every story I write, the baby never does anything, so that when they had things to do, I wrote in there that the mother makes the baby do something. My sister, she doesn't do nothing. She thinks because she is the baby she never does nothing.

I felt good about Tanisha's developing fluency, but I worried about all the historical details that still didn't make sense in her piece. She revised some of the inconsistencies during the course of her writing, but I wanted her to think about others, even if she didn't revise her story again. This was my primary purpose when I conferred with her after she finished her piece.

MS. JORGENSEN: You've done a really nice job on this story. Sometimes it's helpful to look back on something you've written, to think about it again, even though you know you're not going to change it anymore. I thought we could do a little of that today. We've talked a lot about how your piece makes historical sense. Are you wondering about anything in your story that you think might not have happened in 1900?

TANISHA: Probably they wouldn't have balloons for the party.

MS. JORGENSEN: I don't know. That's something you could investigate and find out about.

TANISHA: And in Chapter 5, when the mother asks Timothy and Suzanne to go mail the invitations. What I worried about was, was there all kinds of mail boxes?

MS. JORGENSEN: That's another good historical question. I think that it depended on the town. In some towns, like Berkeley, about 1900, they had home mail delivery. In other places, especially small towns, they didn't. So, as the author, you have to decide how big your town is and whether it makes sense for them to have lots of mail boxes at that time.

Our conversation continued for a few more minutes. Tanisha identified another historical question in her story, and I raised a few that concerned me. We didn't get to every issue, but I was impressed by her ability to think historically. During the course of the ten-week workshop, she had learned to ask whether an idea made historical sense. This was an important accomplishment.

I also talked with her about changes in her sense of history. I was impressed by the number and the variety of resources she consulted to help her write her story. She told me that touching the artifacts helped her understand how it felt to do "old-fashioned chores." She referred to the Bloomingdale's 1886 catalog when she needed clothing ideas and spent several days reading about women's chores in *Women of the West*. And she decided that if she could draw her turn-of-the-century scene again, she would "know what clothing to put on them, how the hats were, the shoes, and the men's vests. And I'd put more things on the street—I'd show streets with railroad track, with railroad tracks in the middle of the street."

A Little Girl And Her Chores

There once was a little girl in theROOS
who had chores to do. She
had to do the dishes by going
out to get some water from a
water pump. For the hot water
she had to bowl some water
and mix it with the cold water
Next she had to srube the floors.
srube
She had to go back out to
the water pump and get some
more water and some sope and
a srub brush and an all around

on the floors srubing. After
srubeing.
that she had to do ironing
she had to put the iron on
a mettle thing and it is
that is
sitting over the fire and the
iron is geting hot. The iron is

Writing Sample 7

hot and now ~~she~~ can ~~begian~~
          She   begins
to iron. When she is finshed
she starts to ~~wors~~ her clothes
                wash
and she washes her clothes by
uscing her hands. After she
is finshed ~~et~~ her clothes
            washing
she starts to hang them.

She hangs her clothes on a
round thing and it has a
long string raped around it
to the other sides ~~and~~ The
other side has another round
thing on it ~~the other side~~. She
leaves the clothes out to
dry and when they dry
                   are
she goes out to get the
clothes and brings them
into the house and folds
them ~~ar~~ puts them away
      and
neatly Then she can have the rest of the day

Writing Sample 7 (continued)

The Girls And There Chores.

Once there was a mother
and she had to little girls. the
              two   The
oldest was Sara she was 11 years
old and Suzanne she was 8 years
old. There mother had to go
far away to get some more food
and it was very far away. She
said it might take two days
said
to get there and back. She
wanted Sara to teach Suzanne
how to do chores so that both
of them can take care of the house.
Suzanne wanted to do chores
sent she was 7 years old but
all her mother kept saying it
                  Kept   was
that when she get's older
she can do chores like Sara.
When Sara told Suzanne that
she had to teach her how

Writing Sample 8

to do chores ~~tt~~ was to she so
happy she could not wate
to begin. Sara said when
mother lives you ~~che~~ can start.
The next day the mother was
geting ready to leave she gave Sara and
Suzanne a kiss and as she
walked out the door they
stood the until they did not
see her. So ~~I~~ Sara closed the
door and her and Suzanne
got to work. Sara said we
will start with the dishes.
Sara told Suzanne to follow
her. To get the cold and hot
water to make worm water you
have to go to the water pump
and that will be ~~tt~~ the cold for
~~wart~~ water and come back and get
another bucket of ~~wart~~ water

Writing Sample 8 (continued)

and that will be for the
hot water. But you have
to boil some water and mix
it to gether. Then after that
we can start to srube the
floors and to do that you
have to come back out to get
some more water and get the
srube brush from out of
the Kiehen and some sape
and just srube m around
all
the fbors. Suzanne seemed to injoy
this and she just could not
wate to start. She asked
Sara when X I start when
can
I finshes teaching you how to
do it. Said Sara. Next after
you do the floors you and I
can do some ironing this is
how we are going to do it but

Writing Sample 8 (continued)

Veun was born in Vietnam. He was energetic and often spoke so quickly in his emerging English that he stumbled over words, creating awkward and sometimes comical phrases. He also walked quickly and smiled a lot. He bubbled with curiosity and didn't hesitate to ask questions about words or concepts he didn't understand. I slowed him down when I talked to him because his mind usually worked faster than his ability to express his ideas in English.

Veun was also a teaching challenge. The native-born children in James's class came to third grade with a significant knowledge of oral and written English and an emerging, somewhat shared historical understanding of the world. This understanding derived from years of interaction with adults, peers, and the American media. Veun came to third grade with a rich knowledge of Vietnamese and an understanding of Southeast Asia and the world that was based on different experiences. I knew the workshop would provide opportunities for him to express his ideas and expand his working knowledge of English, but what about his sense of the past? How could he tell us about it if he spoke limited English? Were there other ways for us to find out? What did he know about the Native American milieu? How was his knowledge affected by his Vietnamese culture?

In October, Veun read *White Bird* with a group that included Lee and Jeff, two Vietnamese boys he played with all the time. Clyde Bulla's novel was a challenge for them, but they worked hard, participating in small-group discussions and keeping up with the daily reading. Veun summarized the plot in his log: "Author tries to talk about how to find the bird." His summary was fairly accurate, and he understood most of the literal details in the story. He also visualized the eighteenth-century milieu, although his picture was sketchy at best. He told James during a group discussion of the book that people in the 1790s didn't have cars. "I think they rode bikes," he commented, "No stop signs." Bikes were common in Vietnam, and I wondered whether that had prompted Veun's response.

I thought that Veun did a good job on the story, although he wasn't sure about the setting for *White Bird*. And his first log entries about the Ohlones were surprising. What would he see if he lived in Ohlone times?

> I think I will see a lot of different trees. I think I will see different animals that I don't know. And I think I will see poor people. And I think the Native Americans go to school. I think they got black skin and black hair and their eyes is blue and they work hard for food. And I think they do all day is pick berries and acorns. I think they hated work. And they went for hunt for animals to eat.

Veun's belief about "school" was the only part that didn't make sense. He wrote later that he believed that the Ohlones dressed in animal skins, and he wanted to know how they "turned it to clothing and what did they wear on their feet?"

Veun's Ohlone milieu drawing contained more unexpected responses than his log entries. He drew an Ohlone village with two buildings, and both buildings had modern roofs and windows. There were no people in sight, and next to the smaller building was a haystack with a pitchfork sticking out of the top. He cut away the wall of a house in another picture, revealing the interior of a room with an Ohlone drill, a gambling game, and five other artifacts lying on shelves and table tops. In the corner of the drawing was a man dressed in a brown garment with a bow and arrow, long black hair, and a hair band with a feather. Veun obviously watched television too, but he modified his understanding quickly. He put more Ohlone artifacts into his pictures than any other student in the classroom. James talked to Veun about his drawing (Figure 3–3).

MR. VENABLE: Tell me more about your Ohlone village.
VEUN: Their country's different there because they hunt animals to eat. A gross thing is that they can't wash it. They don't wash the thing in the water, they wash in the ocean, like animals, tigers and stuff.
MR. VENABLE: What else?
VEUN: They have Indian clothes and shoot animals to eat. They have different houses. I draw a pestle and mortar. I draw everything that the center had when I learned. They speak different language. The Indians speak Native American. The Ohlones speak different kind of language as Indians, but we can't understand it.
MR. VENABLE: What do you think the rest of the world looked like when the Ohlones lived in Alameda?
VEUN: Probably the same.

Veun's sense of the milieu was a mix of expected and unexpected responses. He wasn't sure what the rest of the world looked like, and I found it interesting that he recognized that the Ohlones spoke another language. He was the only student in the class to make that observation, and no doubt his experiences in learning English made him more aware of this issue than the native speakers in the room were.

Veun chose the listening center on the first day of artifact exploration. He heard James tell Ohlone stories but didn't know what to say in his response log: "I am at table 2," he wrote, "but I don't know what to write, so I'll write about table 3." He went on to talk about the animal skins, commenting, "I wonder how do they get the blood and heart and meat out. And I wonder, do they eat the meat and blood and heart or do they throw it away?" This was Veun's third reference to animal skins. I wasn't sure what to make of it, but he seemed interested in this part of Ohlone life.

The next day, Veun's group rotated to the animal-skin center. Veun, Lee, Carl, and Pete spent most of their time examining the pelts. Unlike Sandra's group, the boys did little pretending. Their negotiations were dominated by analytical dialogue. They wondered how the animals were trapped and how the Ohlones prepared the skins. Veun's log entry reflected this conversation: "Do they take off animal and eat it? And why do they don't [sic] take the animal skin off? And why do they cut off the animal ear off? And their claws, and cut bear skin off?"

Veun's interest in the furs continued for several days. He chose to go to the animal-skin center again with a small group of boys. He also read about the animals, noting in his log that the Ohlone hunter put a deer skin over his body to make himself look like an animal so he could "caught the deer."

Veun's fascination with animals surfaced on the first day of storywriting. He wrote about a boy who sneaked out of his hut at night and injured himself after he heard a wolf coming his way (Veun's handwritten draft is included at the end of this section as Writing Sample 9):

The Problem with Mountain Eagle's Going Up to the Mountain

Mountain Eagle want to go up to the mountain, but his mother don't let him go to the mountain because it dangerous. Mountain Eagle friend Air Wolf went to the mountain to get food for his mother. At night, Mountain Eagle snuck out of his room and went to the mountain to find plant to eat when he heard a wolf come his way and he was stuck. He didn't bring his weapon. And he jump off the mountain and he fell in a tree. In the morning, people saw Mountain Eagle fell in a fat tree. And they got him out of the tree and carry him back to their village and put hot water on his face. He woke up, and he saw people around him. People showed him how to shoot arrow. The people's name who showed him how to shoot are Starfish and Starlight and Sunlight.

James and I talked about Veun's first effort. So far, his story made pretty good Ohlone sense. His characters had Ohlone names, they lived in a village, gathered plants to eat, used arrows, and lived with wild animals in a natural setting. Like every other writer in the room, however, Veun's initial work contained several anachronisms and other unexpected responses. But James let him continue writing because he knew he could confer with him later about the historical content of his piece.

By the middle of the second week, Veun's initial page had grown into eight pages of events strung together without a clear focus or story problem. Veun's story was a list of Ohlone events similar in structure to Tanisha's piece about turn-of-the-century household chores. Veun's story, however, made more historical sense than Tanisha's and, despite his limited English, he was a confident and fluent writer. James conferred with Veun to encourage him to organize the piece in a different way.

MR. VENABLE: I read your story last night. It's a very long story, and I got a little confused when I read it. Let's talk about all the different things, or events, that happen in your story. It seems that the first important thing that happens in your story is when the little boy goes up to the mountain and gets hurt. Can you tell me about the next important event?

Figure 3–3

VEUN: When Mountain Eagle got hurt by the lion, he got blood all over him and Starlight was hiding in a bush.

MR. VENABLE: Oh, Starlight finds him. Okay, what other events happened?

VEUN: They carry Mountain Eagle back to the village and put healing plants on him.

MR. VENABLE: I really like the part where they put healing plants on him. Then what happens?

Figure 3–3 (continued)

VEUN: Three people went to pick acorns, but Starfish was the first one to climb up the tree and his basket. He picks acorns in his basket. He saw something that he thought it was an acorn, but it was a squirrel and he laughed and he fell down. He got the squirrel.

MR. VENABLE: So gathering acorns and catching the squirrel was the third thing that happened. Then what happens?

VEUN: Then three people say, "Are you all right?" He just get hurt a little. Then he said, "I'm all right."

MR. VENABLE: Okay, so that was the next important event. What I think you need to do is to think of all the rest of the events in your story, just like we have done together. Then you should read it to other kids and see if there are events in your story that you can leave out, that aren't important. I would be less confused about your story if you took some of the less important events out of it.

Veun spent the next three days revising his piece. Then, on the twelfth day of writing, he abandoned it because he "wanted to write about healing plant." Veun's second piece was a variation on his first story, and it had a clear focus. A boy is injured and villagers use a native plant to heal his wounds. I noticed that wild animals surfaced again in his new story, but I wondered why he had abandoned the first one. In his conference with Veun, James had praised the use of a healing plant to treat Mountain Eagle's injured leg. I suspect that this comment influenced Veun's decision to rethink his Ohlone writing. His new piece began like this (Veun's handwritten draft is included at the end of this section as Writing Sample 10):

The Help of the Healing Plant

There was a boy name Wildstar. He want to go with his dad, but his dad don't let him because danger in the woods. The next day, Wildstar saw no one coming outside, and he snuck to his dad room and he get his dad arrow and bow and his dad was sleep. And he said, "It not scared in the woods." And he went in the woods to hunt deer. He saw two mountain lion, and the two mountain lion one mountain lion claw on his hand and the other scratch his leg. And the man saw Wildstar get hurt by the mountain lion and he got his arrow and bow and he shoot the arrow on the two mountain and the two mountain lion went away in the woods. And the man pick Wildstar up and carrying him into the wood to get healing plant and the men picked some and went back to the village. He get the pestle and the mortar and pounded it to put on Wildstar arm and leg. In a month Wildstar feel better. And the man name was . . .

James saw historical problems in this new piece and used a whole-group share to help Veun try to rethink parts of his story.

MR. VENABLE: What in Veun's story makes good Ohlone sense?
PETE: The healing plant.
MR. VENABLE: Yes, the Ohlones used healing plants. Do you know the name of the healing plant in your story?
VEUN: The one in *White Bird*.
MR. VENABLE: You might want to look at *White Bird* again to find out if they gave it a name. Also, we have plant books that have information about healing plants. Anything else make historical sense?
LOUISA: Animals . . .
MR. VENABLE: Yes, do you remember what kind of animal?
LOUISA: I think, a mountain lion?
MR. VENABLE: Right. What else?
CARL: Use of bow and arrows and stuff . . .

PETE: He said "rooms." I don't think they had rooms.

MR. VENABLE: Good point. That part of the story doesn't make historical sense. What did the Ohlone house look like?

KATHY: It was one room where all the family lived. He could just say that the dad was sleeping in the hut.

VEUN: I could say the house was tule.

MR. VENABLE: Okay. That would make more sense. What about your ending? Have you thought about it?

VEUN: That's when the boy get well and is sorry he left because his father get mad.

The group raised important issues for Veun to consider. Within the next few days, he revised his piece, changing "room" to "lodge" and spending several workshops researching information about which plant to include in his story. James conferred with Veun during this period and showed him how to use the plant resource books.

MR. VENABLE: We had a whole-group share about your new piece last Friday. Did you find the name of a healing plant to use in your story?

VEUN: No, there's none.

MR. VENABLE: Let's look in some books and see if we can find one. (*Goes to center and brings back three native plant books*) There's no table of contents or index, so we'll just look through it and see what we find.

VEUN: I found one, tea medicine.

MR. VENABLE: That's a healing plant, but it's for indigestion.

VEUN: What's that?

MR. VENABLE: Indigestion is when your stomach is upset. Let's keep looking. If we don't find a name, you can call it "healing plant." That'll work just as well. Ah, here's a medicinal plant.

VEUN: What's medicinal plant?

MR. VENABLE: It's a plant that they use for medicine, to help you when you're sick or injured.

VEUN: (*Looking at the book*) Juniper, for sores and cuts.

MR. VENABLE: Here's another one. We have this plant in the room—the alum root.

VEUN: In here? Where?

MR. VENABLE: It's over there at center four. We can look at it in a minute. Look here. It says it was used for sores and swellings. If Wildstar got clawed by a mountain lion, would this be the kind of plant the three men would use to help him?

VEUN: Yes. He got clawed and there was blood.

MR. VENABLE: Okay, you could use the alum root. It says here—help me read—that they pounded the root and used it wet. They used it on sores and swellings—you know how a cut swells or gets big after a while? Here's another one. Yellow root. It was mashed up too. Looks like most of the time they pounded the roots and put it on the sores.

VEUN: These were important plants, wow. How did they know it?

MR. VENABLE: How did the Ohlones know that the plants could help heal them?

VEUN: Yes, how did they know that?

MR. VENABLE: I think they just tried them until one of them worked. They did that for many, many years. Sandocks were used. Look, it says here that the stems and leaves were used as washes for sores. You've got lots of plants you could use. Why don't you make a list of all the plants we've read about and then choose one for your story.

VEUN: Can we go see the root?

MR. VENABLE: Sure, you can make your list later. (*They walk to center four*) Here. This is the alum root. They took a leaf off and pounded it up and put it on the sores when it was still wet with plant juice.

VEUN: This really smells. What about the other plants?

MR. VENABLE: This is the only one that we have.

After his conference with James, Veun brought his list of healing plants to Pete, Carl, and Tim. Later he told me:

> I talked to kids about the healing plant. Then Pete suggest I pick the wild-flower. He look in a book. Carl picked Juniper, and that wasn't that good because it only fix stomachache. The wildflower couldn't do that much good. Tim said alum root. We read about it together, then me and Tim said the alum root.

Veun added "a healing plant called Alum Root" to his story the following day. This seemingly minor revision resulted from days of reading and talking with James and the other writers in the classroom. During these interactions, Veun learned words like "indigestion" and "medicinal" and refined his understanding about Native Americans. His final piece (the handwritten final draft is included as Writing Sample 11) contained many changes, including names for the character that rescued Wildstar:

The Help of the Healing Plant

There was a boy named Wildstar. He wanted to go hunt with his dad but his dad didn't let him because it was dangerous in the woods. The next day Wildstar saw no one coming out side and he sneaked to his dad's lodge and he got his dad's bow and arrows and his dad was asleep. He said, "It's not scary in the woods."

He went in the woods to hunt deer. He saw two mountain lions and the two mountain lions one clawed Wildstar's arm and his hand and the other scratched his leg. The man Fireball saw Wildstar get hurt by the mountain lion and he got his arrow and bow and he shot the arrow at the two mountain lion and the two mountain lion went away in the woods. Fireball picked Wildstar up and carried him out of the wood to get a healing plant called Alum Root and Fireball picked some and went back to his village. He got the pestle and mortar to pound it to put on Wildstar's arm and leg.

In a month, Wildstar felt better. Wildstar thanked Fireball for saving him and Fireball said, "Where is your village?"

"My village is next to the ocean."

Fireball picked him up and carried him to the ocean. And his father saw him and Wildstar learned his lesson. His father thanked Fireball for saving Wildstar's life.

Veun was proud of his work, especially the part about the healing plant. He told me in June that he liked his Ohlone story "because I named the plant Alum Root. Me and Mr. Venable look through it and it said when you really got burned or had a cough or something you put leaf in there and you beat it up with a pestle, and you beat it up and it will be much better." He thought his audience would appreciate his story and also learn that "when you take care of plants, you might have food to eat."

Veun illustrated his book the following week. He included the alum root and the mortar and pestle, but Wildstar and Fireball were clothed in full-length, brown garments, even though we had illustrations in the classroom of Ohlones wearing very little on their bodies. Did Veun's historical understanding change during the course of the workshop? James asked him about his illustrations, hoping to find out what he learned through talking, drawing, and writing about the Ohlones.

MR. VENABLE: Tell me about your illustrations.

VEUN: Here's a tree, and they have a healing plant in there. There's Fireball, and there's the blood.

MR. VENABLE: What are Wildstar and Fireball wearing?

VEUN: You know why I don't want to draw them with no clothes? I don't want to have the kids see that stuff. Without clothes.

MR. VENABLE: I see. What do they have on, then?

VEUN: Here's their clothes. They are string clothes. Here are striped clothes. It's like yarn or string.

MR. VENABLE: How did you come up with that?

VEUN: The Ohlone's make stripes.

MR. VENABLE: What about these Ohlone houses?

VEUN: That's the dad's and the mom's. That's the neighbor's house. Here's the water.

MR. VENABLE: What is this?

VEUN: That's a pestle. The pestle is for pounding something to eat. If someone gets hurt, there's a healing plant to help them. But I don't know if it would because there's fiction story and nonfiction story. Maybe it works. The alum root help headaches and stuff. I found it and drew a picture of it. Ohlones didn't have clothes to wear. Don't have a toilet, they dig a hole.

Veun's new historical understanding was still a mix of expected and unexpected responses. He learned about the healing plant and how the pestle was used but he wondered whether the plant really worked. And James found out that he knew that the Ohlones wore very little clothing, but he was reluctant to draw them that way. He made up "string clothes" using a striped design to make them more Ohlone. His refined Native American milieu included huts, not square buildings with windows. He missed part of the point, however, when he housed the mother and the father in separate lodges.

James used drawings and Veun's emerging English to evaluate his idea of Ohlone history, recognizing the limits of trying to assess complex ideas on the basis of thin and sporadic information. How did Veun's Vietnamese culture affect his learning? James and I never felt we got the whole picture when we talked to Veun. But I think the workshop was important to him because it provided him with an opportunity to talk and write, to learn about a new historical milieu, and to rethink his theories about his experiences in two cultures.

The proldem with Mourtion Eagle is going up to the Mourtion Eagle want to go up to the marrtion but his other don't let him go to the moution because it dengany. Mourtion Eagle friend Air wolf went to the marrtion to get food for his mother. At night Mountian Eagle stct out of his room. And went to the moution to find plan to eat when he hird a wint come his way and he was sack, He diden't bring his wanpen. And he jump off the mourtion and he felling tree. In the maming people saw Mountion Eagle fell in a fat tree. And they got him out of the tree and carry him back to they viglly and put hot water on his face. He wake up and he saw people araund him. People shot him how to short arrow. The people name who reenber him how to short

Writing Sample 9

THE HELP OF THE HEALING PLANTS

Their was a boy name Wild Star he want to go with his dad but his dad don't let him because dunger in the woods. The next day Wild Star saw no one comeing out side and he stik to his dad room. and I get his dad arrow and boom. and his dad was sleep. And he said it not sred in the woods. And he went in the woods to hunt deer he saw two Mountian lion and the two mountian lion one Mountian lion chew hun his hand and the other saie his leg. And the man saw Wild Star get hunt by the mountian lion and he got his arrow and beam and he shoot the arrow on the two mountian and the two mountian lion went away in the woods. And the men pick wild start up and carring him in the wood to get heal plant and the men pick some and went back to the village. He get the the prstle and the mout and pounded it to put on Wild star arm and leg. In a mo Wildstar feel beter. And the men name has

Writing Sample 10

THE HELP OF THE HEALING PLANT

There
Their was a boy named Wild Star. He wanted to go hu
                                                       didn't   it we
with his dad but his dad don't let him because is
unger in the woods. The next day Wild Star saw nooooe
                               break   lodge
omeing out side and he (it it) to his dad's log and he
                                              ing
ot his dads bow and arrows and his dad was asleepn And
              scary
said, "It's not (saed) in the woods." He went
he woods to hunt deer. He saw two Mountian lionsand
                                                     wild star
he two mountianlions one Mountianlion chaues ann
                         scratch   *   maa use
's hand and the other (sare) his leg. And the
    well
aw Wildstar got hurt by the mountian lion and he
                                        shot
ot his arrow and bown and he shoot the arrow
                     lion
it the two mountiana and the two mountian lion
                                  Fireball
ent away in the woods. And its men picked Wild Star
                 Fireball
Yuni root and the men picked some and went back to
his
the village. He got the the pestle and the (mortal mouv) ite
                                                        mortal
pounded it to put on Wild star's arm and leg. Tha mort
       felt
Wildstar feel better. And the men name was fireball
                            Fireball
t Wildstar thanked the men for safting him
            Fireball
and this these said, "Where is your village? "My Villa

Writing Sample 11

is next to the ocean ~~Fireball~~ picked him up and carried him

carring to sthe ocean. And his father saw him

and Wildstar learned his lesson A. His father

thanked for saftn Fireball my wild Stars life.

The End

THE END

Writing Sample 11 (continued)

Afterword
. . . .

I find myself wondering about a lot of issues as I look back at my work during the last three years. I wonder, for instance, if the workshop setting would work if we focused on world history. After all, artifacts and books are fairly easy to obtain for the late nineteenth century and for Native American studies. What would happen if we studied ancient Egypt, nineteenth-century China, or modern Africa? Could I find artifacts? Do I need any, and, if so, how many?

I also wonder if I could structure the workshop to give students more choices. James is particularly concerned about this point. He thinks we should set up one or two centers based on student interests and simply let the students explore, choose genres, and write if and when they are ready. He thinks he could stimulate historical writing by reading historical fiction and expository pieces aloud and by modeling different historical genres in his own writing. He also wants to broaden the range of language experiences in the workshop to include more myths, poetry, and music. This makes sense to me. I think it would enrich the workshop and strengthen the children's voices, creating a better power balance between us.

The history response logs are still a problem for me. We tried them several different ways in James's third- and fourth-grade classes, and I did something slightly different in Janet's fifth-grade classroom. Some children use them and others don't. I find them useful for assessment, since they help me stay in touch with the daily activities of the workshop, but they certainly can't stand on their own. I need to supplement response log observations with other information in order to see the whole picture. Would the response logs work better if we too commented in the logs, carrying on a conversation just as we do in conferences and minilessons? I need to experiment with this.

And what about expository writing? Cynthia Brown and I discussed the differences between expository and narrative writing at length, believing that young children responded more enthusiastically to stories than to analysis or descriptions. But now I'm not sure about the relationship between exposition and narrative. It's more complicated than I thought. Children love to hear stories, but they have a hard time writing good ones. Descriptive expository writing is often boring for them to read, but many can write it with relative ease. What's the connection between narrative and expository writing? What's the connection between reading and writing narrative? I want to find out.

A student named Margaret presented another puzzle. In our final conference, she told me that Lizzy, a character in her story, was modeled after a favorite doll. She said she had a hard time "seeing" the other characters in her piece, but not Lizzy. Lizzy was special, and when Lizzy talked, Margaret felt she was inside her story, talking out of Lizzy's mouth, seeing out of Lizzy's eyes. As I listened to Margaret, I thought about how our children wrote fiction. They were event-oriented, forming stories around a series of actions performed by flat, motiveless cartoon characters. I think we reinforced this tendency by focusing many of our conferences and minilessons on story problems and other plot-related issues. What about character development? I sense that young writers are able to develop vital characters who act like real people. But what can I do to help them "see" characters in the way that Margaret saw Lizzy? And if they see characters this way, does it mean that they also empathize with real people living in those historical times? I want to know this, too.

In some ways my experiences during the last three years have raised as many questions as they've answered. But I'm not disturbed by this because I see teaching as an ongoing experiment, as a perpetual search for new ideas about the nature of learning. I plan to continue listening, watching, and talking with my students, modifying the history workshop as I learn more about how children use language to understand the world.

Works Cited

Bloomingdale's Illustrated 1886 Catalog. New York: Dover, 1988.

Bulla, Clyde. *A Lion to Guard Us.* New York: Harper, 1981.

———. *White Bird.* New York: MacKay, 1990.

Calkins, Lucy. *The Art of Teaching Writing.* Portsmouth, NH: Heinemann, 1986.

Carrick, Carol. *Stay Away from Simon.* New York: Clarion, 1985.

Coerr, Elizabeth. *Sadako and a Thousand Paper Cranes.* New York: Putnam, 1977.

Goodman, Ken, and Yetta Goodman. *The Whole Language Evaluation Book.* Portsmouth, NH: Heinemann, 1989.

Goodman, Yetta. *Reading Miscue Inventory.* New York: Richard C. Owens, 1987.

Graves, Donald. *Writing: Teachers and Children at Work.* Portsmouth, NH: Heinemann, 1983.

Harste, Jerome, et. al. *Creating Classrooms for Authors.* Portsmouth, NH: Heinemann, 1988.

Holdaway, Don. *Independence in Reading,* 3d ed. Portsmouth, NH: Heinemann, 1991.

Hutchins, Pat. *Rosie's Walk.* New York: MacMillan, 1968.

Knope, Terry. *The Adventures of Little Bird.* Berkeley, CA: Images, 1984.

Lobel, Arnold. *Frog and Toad Together.* New York: Harper Junior, 1970.

Luchetti, Cathy. *Women of the West.* St. George: Antelope Island, 1982.

Macaulay, David. *Castle.* New York: Houghton Mifflin, 1977.

MacLachlan, Patricia. *Sarah, Plain and Tall*. New York: Harper, 1987.

Margolin, Malcolm. *The Ohlone Way*. Berkeley, CA: Heyday, 1978.

Phinney, Margaret. *Reading with the Troubled Reader*. Portsmouth, NH: Heinemann, 1988.

Seldon, George. *Cricket in Times Square*. New York: Dell, 1970.

Shub, Elizabeth, *The White Stallion*. New York: Greenwillow, 1982.

Slobodkina, Esphyr. *Caps for Sale*. Harper Junior, 1947.

Stevens, Carla. *Anna and the Big Storm*. New York: Clarion, 1982.

Wilder, Laura Ingalls. *Little House in the Big Woods*. New York: Harper Junior, 1953.

Pictorial Bibliography:
Historical Photographs, Illustrations, and Films Documenting United States History

Abbott, Bernice. *New York in the Thirties*. New York: Dover, 1973. Photographs capturing life in New York City during the Great Depression.

Bloomingdale's Illustrated 1886 Catalog. New York: Dover, 1988. A facsimile edition mail order catalog showing late-nineteenth-century clothing and personal accessories.

Blum, Stella, ed. *Everyday Fashions of the Thirties as Pictured in Sears Catalogs*. New York: Dover, 1986. A compilation of illustrations from Sears mail order catalogs depicting clothing worn during the 1930s.

————. *Everyday Fashions of the Twenties as Pictured in Sears and Other Catalogs*. New York: Dover, 1982. A compilation of illustrations from mail order catalogs depicting clothing worn during the 1920s.

Catalog of Historical and Other Films: 1894–1915. Hollywood, CA,: Historical Films, n.d., 1982. Listing of the Library of Congress's collection of motion pictures shot in the United States from 1894 to 1915. For catalog and film order form, write to Historical Films, P.O. Box 46505, Hollywood, CA 90046.

Easter, Eric, ed. *Songs of My People*. Boston: Little, Brown, 1992. Photographs documenting African American life in cities throughout the United States in 1990.

Feininger, Andreas. *Industrial America*. New York: Dover, 1982. Photographs showing life in the United States from 1940 to 1960.

Freedman, Russell. *Children of the Wild West*. New York: Clarion, 1983. Children's book using photographs and text to document how young people lived in the West from 1850 to 1900.

————. *Immigrant Kids*. New York: Dutton, 1980. Children's book using photographs taken by Jacob Riis and others to show how young immigrants lived in New York City during the 1880s.

————. *Indian Chiefs*. New York: Holiday House, 1987. Children's book using photographs and text to illustrate Native American life from 1870 to 1900.

Gernsheim, Alison. *Victorian and Edwardian Fashion*. New York: Dover, 1981. Photographs depicting nineteenth- and early-twentieth-century fashion.

Harter, Jim. *Food and Drink: A Pictorial Archive from Nineteenth-Century Sources*. New York: Dover, 1983. Wood engravings from the 1880s and 1890s illustrating food, drink, manners, and cooking utensils.

————. *Transportation: A Pictorial Archive from Nineteenth-Century Sources*. New York: Dover, 1984. Wood engravings documenting nineteenth- and early-twentieth-century modes of transportation.

Heilman, Grant. *Farm Town: A Memoir of the 1930s*. Lexington, KY: Stephen Greene, 1987. Photographs showing life in a small rural Kansas community during the Great Depression.

Kuo Wei Tchen, John. *Genthe's Photographs of San Francisco's Old Chinatown*. New York: Dover, 1984. Photographs by Arnold Genthe affording a view of Chinese life in San Francisco from 1895 to 1906.

Luchetti, Cathy. *Women of the West*. St George: Antelope Island, 1982. Photographs, diary excerpts, and letters telling stories of women in the West from 1850 to 1900.

Mace, O. Henry. *Collector's Guide to Early Photographs*. Radnor, PA: Wallace-Homestead, 1990. A history of photography from 1839 to 1900.

Meredith, Roy. *Mr. Lincoln's Camera Man, Mathew B. Brady*. New York: Dover, 1974. Mathew Brady's early photographs, including those of Abraham Lincoln and scenes from the Civil War period.

Motion Pictures from the Library of Congress Paper Print Collection, 1894–1912. Berkeley, CA: University of California, 1967. Detailed listing of vintage film footage available through the Historical Films company.

National Archives and Record Service. *The American Image: Photographs from the National Archives, 1869–1960*. New York: Pantheon, 1979. Selected photographs from the National Archives.

Newhall, Beaumont. *History of Photography*. New York: Museum of Modern Art, 1982. A comprehensive history of photography from 1839 to the twentieth century.

Riis, Jacob. *How the Other Half Lives: Studies Among Tenements of New York*. New York: Dover, 1971. Photographs by Jacob Riis documenting working-class immigrant life in New York City during the 1880s.

Rothstein, Arthur. *The Depression Years as Photographed by Arthur Rothstein*. New York, Dover, 1978. Rothstein's photographs showing life in the United States during the Great Depression.

The Small Town Sourcebook, Part I. Sturbridge, MA: Old Sturbridge Village, 1979. Photographs, wood engravings, drawings, maps, and paintings depicting life in a rural Massachusetts village during the 1820s on through the early twentieth century.

Steltzer, Ulli. *The New Americans.* Pasadena, CA: New Sage, 1988. Photographs documenting lives of recent Asian and Hispanic immigrants in Southern California in the 1980s.

Stryker, Roy, and Nancy Wood. *In This Proud Land: America 1935–1943 as Seen in the FSA Photographs.* New York: Galahad, 1973. Photographs showing life in the United States during the Great Depression and the early years of World War II.

Ward, Baldwin, ed. *Pictorial History of the Black American.* New York: YEAR, 1968. Photographs, paintings, wood engravings, and drawings depicting the history of African Americans in the United States from slavery through the twentieth century.

Wolf, Bernard. *In This Proud Land.* New York: Harper, 1979. Photographs and text documenting the life of a contemporary Mexican American family who live in Mexico and migrate yearly to do farm work in Texas.

KAREN JORGENSEN

*has spent the last fourteen years studying
how children develop historical literacy.
Her observations are based on her experiences
as a parent and as a classroom and resource
teacher. She has published numerous articles
and curriculum guides in the area of
history–social studies and holds a doctorate
in education from the University of California.
She currently teaches reading and writing in
a multiethnic setting at Washington School
in Alameda, California. She lives in Berkeley
with her three teenage children.*

. . . .

JAMES W. VENABLE

*is a teacher-researcher committed to
full-time classroom instruction.
He has taught and observed children at the
K–5 level for sixteen years in Louisville,
Kentucky, and in the San Francisco Bay Area.
He values collaboration and serves as a mentor
for his colleagues at Washington School
in Alameda, California.*